RECIPES FOR
SOUPS

A Collection of Timeless
and Trusted Recipes

hamlyn

CONTENTS

INTRODUCTION

Aromatic, brimming with fresh ingredients and the perfect pick-me-up for body and mind, homemade soup puts a hug in a mug or soul in a bowl.

Soups are far greater than the sum of their parts. A dash of cream, a spinkle of herbs or a simmer with a few aromatic spices will transform the most humble ingredients into something extraordinary.

In this collection of over 80 recipes, you'll find soups for all moods, seasons and occasions. There are banquet-worthy bisques and Bouillabaisses, Asian-inspired broths bursting with fiery ginger and fragrant lemongrass; comforting classics and hearty mains and plenty of recipe suggestions for things to dunk, dip or scatter on top.

The secret to a sensational soup is the stock. The Basics section overleaf contains a few stock recipes to get you started. All can be made ahead of time and kept in the fridge for up to three days or frozen for up to six months. If you're using stock cubes, make them up with a little extra water so that their flavour is not overpowering. Tubs of chilled ready-made stocks are readily available and are much closer to the taste of homemade stock.

THE BASICS

CHICKEN STOCK

MAKES about
1 litre (1¾ pints)

1 leftover cooked chicken
  carcass
1 onion, quartered
2 carrots, thickly sliced
2 celery sticks, thickly sliced
1 bay leaf or small bunch of
  mixed herbs
¼ teaspoon salt
½ teaspoon roughly crushed
  black peppercorns
2.5 litres (4 pints) cold water

VEGETABLE STOCK

MAKES about
1 litre (1¾ pints)

1 tablespoon olive oil
2 onions, roughly chopped
2 leek tops, roughly chopped
4 carrots, roughly chopped
2 celery sticks, thickly sliced
100 g (3½ oz) cup
  mushrooms, sliced
4 tomatoes, roughly
  chopped
small bunch of mixed herbs
½ teaspoon roughly crushed
  black peppercorns
¼ teaspoon salt
1.8 litres (3 pints) cold water

BEEF STOCK

MAKES about
1 litre (1¾ pints)

2 kg (4 lb) beef bones, such
  as ribs or shin
2 smoked streaky bacon
  rashers, diced
2 onions, quartered but
  with the inner brown
  layer still on
2 carrots, thickly sliced
2 celery sticks, thickly sliced
1 turnip, diced (optional)
2 bay leaves, rosemary sprigs
  or sage stems
¼ teaspoon salt
½ teaspoon roughly crushed
  black peppercorns
3.6 litres (6 pints) cold water

FISH STOCK

MAKES about
1 litre (1¾ pints)

1 kg (2 lb) fish trimmings,
  such as backbones, skins
  and prawn shells, rinsed in
  a sieve and drained
1 onion, quartered
2 leek tops, sliced
2 carrots, thickly sliced
2 celery sticks, thickly sliced
a few thyme sprigs
1 bay leaf
a few parsley stalks
½ teaspoon roughly crushed
  white peppercorns
¼ teaspoon salt
1.5 litres (2½ pints) cold water
300 ml (½ pint) dry white
  wine or extra water

CHICKEN STOCK – add all the ingredients to a large saucepan and bring slowly to the boil. Skim off any scum with a slotted spoon. Reduce the heat to a gentle simmer, then cook for 2–2½ hours until reduced by about half. Strain the stock through a large sieve. Reserve any chicken pieces still on the carcass and in the sieve for the soup, but discard the vegetables. A DUCK or PHEASANT carcass or a HAM knuckle can be made into stock in just the same way.

VEGETABLE STOCK – heat the oil in a large saucepan, add the vegetables and fry for 5 minutes. Add the tomatoes, herbs, peppercorns and salt. Pour in the water, slowly bring to the boil, then half cover and simmer gently for 1 hour. Strain through a sieve.

BEEF STOCK – put the bones and bacon into a large saucepan and heat gently for 10 minutes. Add the vegetables and fry for 10 more minutes. Add the herbs, salt and peppercorns, then pour in the water and bring slowly to the boil. Skim off any scum with a slotted spoon, then reduce the heat and simmer gently for 4–5 hours until the liquid has reduced by half. Strain through a large sieve into a jug.

LAMB STOCK – made in the same way as beef stock, using cooked or uncooked lamb bones.

FISH STOCK – put the fish trimmings into a large saucepan with all the remaining ingredients. Bring slowly to the boil. Skim off any scum with a slotted spoon. Cover and simmer for 30 minutes. Strain the stock through a fine sieve, return it to the saucepan and then simmer it, uncovered, for about 15 minutes until reduced by half.

THE
CLASSICS

MINESTRONE

SERVES 4
PREPARATION TIME 5 minutes
COOKING TIME 23 minutes

2 tablespoons olive oil
1 onion, chopped
1 garlic clove, crushed
2 celery sticks, chopped
1 leek, finely sliced
1 carrot, chopped
400 g (13 oz) can chopped
   tomatoes
600 ml (1 pint) chicken
   or vegetable stock
   (see pages 7–9)

1 courgette, diced
½ small cabbage, shredded
1 bay leaf
75 g (3 oz) canned haricot
   beans, drained and rinsed
75 g (3 oz) small pasta shapes
1 tablespoon chopped flat-leaf
   parsley
salt and pepper
grated Parmesan, to serve

Heat the oil in a large saucepan. Add the onion, garlic, celery, leek and carrot and cook over a medium heat, stirring occasionally, for 5 minutes. Add the tomatoes, stock, courgette, cabbage, bay leaf and haricot beans. Bring to the boil, reduce the heat and simmer for 10 minutes.

Add the pasta and season to taste. Stir well and cook for a further 8 minutes. Keep stirring, as the soup may stick to the base of the pan. Just before serving, add the parsley and stir well. Ladle into bowls and serve with grated Parmesan.

FRENCH ONION SOUP

SERVES 4
PREPARATION TIME 15 minutes
COOKING TIME 1 hour

25 g (1 oz) butter
2 tablespoons olive oil
500 g (1 lb) large onions,
    halved and thinly sliced
1 tablespoon caster sugar
3 tablespoons brandy
150 ml (¼ pint) red wine
1 litre (1¾ pints) beef stock
    (see pages 7–9)

1 bay leaf
salt and pepper

**FOR THE CHEESY
CROÛTES**
4–8 slices of French bread
1 garlic clove, halved
40 g (1½ oz) Gruyère, grated

Heat the butter and oil in a saucepan, add the onions and toss in the butter, then fry very gently for 20 minutes, stirring occasionally until very soft and just beginning to turn golden around the edges.

Stir in the sugar and fry the onions for 20 minutes more, stirring more frequently towards the end of cooking until the onions are caramelized to a rich dark brown. Add the brandy and, when bubbling, flame with a long match and quickly stand back.

Add the wine, stock, bay leaf, salt and pepper as soon as the flames subside, then bring to the boil. Cover and simmer for 20 minutes. Taste and adjust the seasoning if needed.

Make the croûtes. Toast the bread on both sides, then rub with the cut surface of the garlic. Sprinkle with the cheese and put back under the grill until the cheese is bubbling. Ladle the soup into bowls and top with the cheesy croûtes.

COCK-A-LEEKIE SOUP

SERVES 6
PREPARATION TIME 30 minutes
COOKING TIME 2 hours

1 tablespoon sunflower oil
2 chicken thigh and leg joints
(about 375 g / 12 oz)
500 g (1 lb) leeks, thinly sliced,
white and green parts kept
separate
3 smoked streaky bacon
rashers, diced

2.5 litres (4 pints) chicken
stock (see pages 7–9)
75 g (3 oz) stoned prunes,
quartered
1 bay leaf
1 large thyme sprig
50 g (2 oz) long-grain rice
salt and pepper

Heat the oil in a large saucepan, add the chicken joints and fry on one side until golden. Turn them over and add the white sliced leeks and bacon. Fry until the chicken is golden all over and the leeks and bacon just beginning to colour.

Pour in the stock, then add the prunes, bay leaf and thyme, season with salt and pepper and bring to the boil. Cover and simmer for 1½ hours, stirring occasionally until the chicken is falling off the bones.

Lift the chicken, bay leaf and thyme out of the soup with a slotted spoon and put on a plate (discard the herbs). Remove the skin and bones from the chicken, then cut the meat into pieces. Return the chicken to the pan, adding the rice and green leek slices. Simmer for 10 minutes until the rice and leeks are tender.

Taste and adjust the seasoning if needed. Ladle the soup into bowls and serve with warm, crusty bread.

CREAM OF CHICKEN SOUP

SERVES 6
PREPARATION TIME 30 minutes
COOKING TIME 2 hours

1 tablespoon sunflower oil
2 chicken thigh and leg joints,
    (about 375 g / 12 oz)
500 g (1 lb) leeks, thinly sliced,
    white and green parts kept
    separate
3 smoked streaky bacon
    rashers, diced

2 litres (3½ pints) chicken
    stock (see pages 7–9)
250 g (8 oz) potato, diced
1 bay leaf
1 large thyme sprig
150 ml (¼ pint) milk
150 ml (¼ pint) double cream
salt and pepper
croûtons, to serve

Heat the oil in a large saucepan, add the chicken joints and fry on one side until golden. Turn them over and add the white sliced leeks and bacon. Fry until the chicken is golden all over and the leeks and bacon just beginning to colour.

Pour in the stock, then add the potato, bay leaf and thyme, season with salt and pepper and bring to the boil. Cover and simmer for 1½ hours, stirring occasionally until the chicken is falling off the bones.

Lift the chicken, bay leaf and thyme sprigs out of the soup with a slotted spoon and put on a plate (discard the herbs). Remove the skin and bones from the chicken, then cut the meat into pieces. Return the chicken to the pan, adding the green leek slices. Simmer for 10 minutes until the leeks are tender.

Allow the soup to cool slightly, then purée in batches in a blender or food processor. Pour back into the saucepan and stir in the milk and cream. Reheat, but take care to bring just to the boil and then reduce the heat to a simmer, stirring until hot all the way through.

Taste and adjust the seasoning if needed. Ladle the soup into bowls and serve with croûtons.

MULLIGATAWNY SOUP

SERVES 6
PREPARATION TIME 15 minutes
COOKING TIME about 1¼ hours

1 tablespoon sunflower oil
1 onion, finely chopped
1 carrot, diced
1 dessert apple, peeled, cored and diced
2 garlic cloves, finely chopped
250 g (8 oz) tomatoes, roughly chopped
4 teaspoons curry paste

50 g (2 oz) sultanas
125 g (4 oz) dried red lentils, rinsed
1.5 litres (2½ pints) chicken stock (see pages 7–9)
125 g (4 oz) leftover cooked chicken, shredded
salt and pepper
coriander sprigs, to garnish

Heat the oil in a saucepan, add the onion and carrot and fry for 5 minutes, stirring until softened and just turning golden around the edges. Stir in the apple, garlic, tomatoes and curry paste and cook for 2 minutes.

Stir in the sultanas, lentils and stock. Season with salt and pepper and bring to the boil, cover and simmer for 1 hour until the lentils are soft. Mash the soup to make a coarse purée. Add the cooked chicken, heat thoroughly, then taste and adjust the seasoning if needed.

Ladle into bowls and garnish with coriander sprigs. Serve with warm naan bread or poppadums.

CLASSIC VICHYSSOISE

SERVES 6
PREPARATION TIME 20 minutes
COOKING TIME 30 minutes + chilling

25 g (1 oz) butter
375 g (12 oz) leeks, sliced
150 g (5 oz) potato, diced
450 ml (¾ pint) chicken stock
   (see pages 7–9)

250 ml (8 fl oz) milk
150 ml (¼ pint) double cream
salt and pepper
chives, to garnish

Heat the butter in a saucepan, add the leeks and potato, toss in the butter, then cover and fry gently for 10 minutes, stirring occasionally until softened but not browned.

Pour in the stock, season and bring to the boil. Cover and simmer for 15 minutes until the vegetables are just tender.

Allow the soup to cool slightly, then purée in batches in a blender or food processor until smooth. Pour the purée through a fine sieve back into the saucepan, then press the coarser pieces of leeks through the sieve using the back of a ladle. Mix in the milk and half the cream, then taste and adjust the seasoning if needed. Chill well.

Ladle the soup into small bowls, swirl the rest of the cream through the soup and garnish with a sprinkling of a few snipped chives before serving.

MUSHROOM SOUP

SERVES 4
PREPARATION TIME 10 minutes
COOKING TIME 15–20 minutes

25 g (1 oz) butter
1 large onion, chopped
1 leek, finely sliced
2 garlic cloves, crushed
300 g (10 oz) chestnut
   mushrooms, roughly
   chopped

2 tablespoons plain flour
500 ml (17 fl oz) vegetable
   stock (see pages 7–9)
400 ml (14 fl oz) milk
1 tablespoon tarragon,
   finely chopped
salt and pepper

Melt the butter in a pan over a low heat and gently fry the onion, leek and garlic until they start to soften.

Increase the heat and add the mushrooms to the pan, stirring until well combined. Continue to fry, stirring, for 2–3 minutes. Stir in the flour and continue to cook for 1 minute. Remove the pan from the heat and add the stock a little at a time, stirring well between each addition.

Once all the stock is added, return the pan to the heat, bring to the boil, reduce the heat and simmer for a few minutes. Pour in the milk and bring to a simmer. Stir in the tarragon and season to taste. Ladle the soup into bowls and serve with crusty bread.

TOMATO & BREAD SOUP

SERVES 4
PREPARATION TIME 10 minutes
COOKING TIME 35 minutes

1 kg (2 lb) really ripe vine tomatoes, skinned, deseeded and chopped

300 ml (½ pint) vegetable stock (see pages 7–9)

6 tablespoons extra virgin olive oil

2 garlic cloves, crushed

1 teaspoon sugar

2 tablespoons chopped basil

100 g (3½ oz) ciabatta bread

1 tablespoon balsamic vinegar

salt and pepper

basil leaves, to garnish

Place the tomatoes in a saucepan with the stock, 2 tablespoons of the oil, the garlic, sugar and basil and gradually bring to the boil. Cover the pan and simmer gently for 30 minutes.

Crumble the bread into the soup and stir over a low heat until it has thickened. Stir in the vinegar and the remaining oil, and season with salt and pepper to taste. Serve immediately or leave to cool to room temperature, if preferred. Garnish with basil leaves.

BASQUE FISH SOUP

SERVES 6
PREPARATION TIME 20 minutes
COOKING TIME 45 minutes

2 tablespoons olive oil
1 onion, finely chopped
½ green pepper, cored,
    deseeded and diced
½ red pepper, cored,
    deseeded and diced
1 courgette, diced
2 garlic cloves, finely chopped
250 g (8 oz) potatoes, cut into
    chunks
½ teaspoon smoked paprika

150 ml (¼ pint) red wine
1 litre (1¾ pints) fish stock
    (see pages 7–9)
400 g (13 oz) can chopped
    tomatoes
1 tablespoon tomato purée
2 whole mackerel, gutted,
    rinsed with cold water
    inside and out
salt and cayenne pepper

Heat the oil in a large saucepan, add the onion and fry gently for 5 minutes until softened. Add the peppers, courgette, garlic and potato and fry for 5 minutes, stirring. Mix in the paprika and cook for 1 minute.

Pour in the red wine, stock, tomatoes, tomato purée, and season with salt and cayenne pepper. Bring to the boil, stirring, then add the whole mackerel. Cover and simmer gently for 20 minutes until the fish flakes easily when pressed with a knife.

Lift the fish out with a slotted spoon and put on a plate. Simmer the soup, uncovered, for a further 15 minutes. Peel the skin off the fish, then lift the flesh away from the backbone. Flake into pieces, checking carefully for any bones.

Return the mackerel flakes to the pan. Reheat and ladle into shallow bowls. Serve with lemon wedges and crusty bread.

CHEAT'S BOUILLABAISSE WITH ROUILLE

SERVES 6
PREPARATION TIME 15 minutes
COOKING TIME 30 minutes

2 tablespoons olive oil

1 large onion, finely chopped

1 leek, thinly sliced

2 large pinches of saffron threads

2 garlic cloves, finely chopped

500 g (1 lb) plum tomatoes, skinned, roughly chopped

150 ml (¼ pint) dry white wine

600 ml (1 pint) fish stock (see pages 7–9)

2–3 thyme stems, leaves torn from stems

500 g (1 lb) firm white fish (monkfish, hake, haddock or cod), skinned and cubed

400 g (13 oz) frozen mixed seafood, defrosted, rinsed with cold water and drained

salt and pepper

½ small French bread, sliced and toasted

FOR THE ROUILLE

3 roasted red peppers from a jar, drained

2–3 garlic cloves

1 teaspoon finely chopped red chilli (from a jar)

1 slice of white bread, torn into pieces

pinch of saffron threads, soaked in 1 tablespoon hot water, then drained

3 tablespoons olive oil

Heat the oil in a large saucepan, add the onion and leek and fry gently for 5 minutes, stirring until softened. Meanwhile soak the saffron in 1 tablespoon hot water, then drain.

Add the garlic and tomatoes to the pan and fry for 2–3 minutes, then mix in the soaked saffron, wine, stock, thyme and season with salt and pepper. Cover and simmer for 10 minutes.

Add the white fish, re-cover and simmer gently for 3 minutes. Add the mixed seafood, re-cover and simmer gently for 5 more minutes until all the fish is just cooked.

Make the rouille. Put the peppers in a blender or food processor with the garlic, chilli, bread, saffron and oil. Blend until smooth.

Ladle into bowls and serve with toasted bread topped with spoonfuls of rouille.

CRAB BISQUE

SERVES 6
PREPARATION TIME 20 minutes
COOKING TIME 25 minutes

25 g (1 oz) butter
1 onion, roughly chopped
2 tablespoons brandy
40 g (1½ oz) long-grain rice
300 ml (½ pint) fish stock
   (see pages 7–9)
150 g (5 oz) prepared crab in
   the shell, plus 1 extra crab,
   to garnish (optional)

2 canned anchovy fillets,
   drained and chopped
½ teaspoon mild paprika
200 ml (7 fl oz) milk
150 ml (¼ pint) double cream
salt and cayenne pepper

Heat the butter in a saucepan, add the onion and fry gently for 5 minutes until softened. Add the brandy and when boiling, flame with a long match and quickly stand back. As soon as the flames have subsided, stir in the rice and add the stock.

Scoop the dark and white crab meat out of the shell into the pan, then mix in the anchovies and paprika. Season with a little salt and cayenne pepper, then bring to the boil. Cover and simmer for 20 minutes.

Allow the soup to cool slightly, then purée in batches in a blender or food processor. Pour back into the saucepan and stir in the milk and cream. Reheat, but take care to bring just to the boil, then reduce the heat to a simmer, stirring until hot all the way through. Taste and adjust the seasoning if needed.

Pour into teacups. Pick out the crab meat from the extra crab (if using) and flake into pieces. Serve in a separate bowl for diners to sprinkle over their soup and garnish with a little extra paprika.

SCOTTISH CULLEN SKINK

SERVES 6
PREPARATION TIME 25 minutes
COOKING TIME 40 minutes

25 g (1 oz) butter
1 onion, roughly chopped
500 g (1 lb) potatoes, diced
1 large Finnan haddock or
    300 g (10 oz) smoked
    haddock fillet
1 bay leaf

900 ml (1½ pints) fish stock
    (see pages 7–9)
150 ml (¼ pint) milk
6 tablespoons double cream
salt and pepper
chopped parsley, to garnish

Heat the butter in a saucepan, add the onion and fry gently for 5 minutes until softened. Stir in the potatoes, then cover and cook for 5 more minutes. Lay the haddock on top, add the bay leaf and stock. Season with salt and pepper and bring to the boil.

Cover and simmer for 30 minutes, or until the potatoes are soft. Lift the fish out of the pan with a slotted spoon and transfer to a plate. Discard the bay leaf.

Loosen the bones, if using a Finnan haddock, with a small knife, then lift away the backbone and head. Use a knife and fork to break the fish into flakes and lift off the skin. If using haddock fillet, simply peel off the skin and then break the fish into flakes, double-checking there are no bones.

Return two-thirds of the fish to the pan, then purée the soup in batches in a blender or food processor until smooth. Pour back into the saucepan and stir in the milk and cream. Bring just to the boil, then simmer gently until reheated. Taste and adjust the seasoning if needed.

Ladle into bowls, sprinkle with the remaining fish and the parsley. Serve with toasted barley bannocks or soda griddle scones.

SPICED SQUASH SOUP

SERVES 8
PREPARATION TIME 15 minutes
COOKING TIME 1 hour and 10 minutes

2 tablespoons flavourless oil
1 large red onion, roughly sliced
3 garlic cloves, roughly sliced
25 g (1 oz) root ginger, peeled and roughly chopped
1 tablespoon mild curry powder
3 tablespoons vegetable bouillon powder
1 litre (1¾ pints) water
1 large butternut squash (about 1 kg / 2 lb), peeled, deseeded and roughly chopped

200 g (7 oz) can coconut milk, 2 tablespoons reserved to garnish
2–3 tablespoons lime juice
salt and pepper

TO SERVE
1 red chilli, deseeded and finely sliced
large handful of coriander, roughly chopped
2 tablespoons sesame seeds

Heat the oil in a large saucepan or casserole dish over a medium heat, add the onion and fry for 6–8 minutes until golden and starting to soften. Add the garlic and ginger and fry for 2 minutes, then add the curry powder, stir well and cook for 1 minute.

Add the bouillon powder with the measured water and the squash. Bring to the boil, then reduce the heat to a simmer and cover with a lid. Cook for 1 hour, until the squash is tender when pierced with a fork.

Add the coconut milk and use a hand blender to blitz the soup until smooth, or allow to cool and use a food processor or blender.

Stir in the lime juice and season with salt and pepper. Swirl in the reserved coconut milk and serve with the red chilli slices, coriander and sesame seeds, either scattered on top or in bowls on the side for people to help themselves to.

MAINS

BEEF & BARLEY BROTH

SERVES 6
PREPARATION TIME 20 minutes
COOKING TIME 2 hours

25 g (1 oz) butter
250 g (8 oz) braising beef, fat
   trimmed away and meat
   cut into small cubes
1 large onion, finely chopped
200 g (7 oz) swede, diced
150 g (5 oz) carrot, diced

100 g (3½ oz) pearl barley
2 litres (3½ pints) beef stock
   (see pages 7–9)
2 teaspoons English mustard
   powder (optional)
salt and pepper
chopped parsley, to garnish

Heat the butter in a large saucepan, add the beef and onion and fry for 5 minutes, stirring, until the beef is browned and the onion just beginning to colour.

Stir in the diced vegetables, pearl barley, stock and mustard powder, if using. Season with salt and pepper and bring to the boil. Cover and simmer for 1¾ hours, stirring occasionally until the meat and vegetables are very tender. Taste and adjust the seasoning if needed. Ladle the soup into bowls and sprinkle with a little chopped parsley. Serve with warm potato bannocks or farls.

BEER BROTH WITH MINI MEATBALLS

SERVES 6
PREPARATION TIME 25 minutes
COOKING TIME about 1¼ hours

25 g (1 oz) butter
1 onion, chopped
200 g (7 oz) potato, diced
125 g (4 oz) swede or parsnip, diced
1 carrot, diced
2 tomatoes, skinned if liked, roughly chopped
½ lemon, sliced
900 ml (1½ pints) beef stock (see pages 7–9)
450 ml (¾ pint) can lager
¼ teaspoon ground cinnamon

¼ teaspoon grated nutmeg
100 g (3½ oz) green cabbage, finely shredded
salt and pepper

FOR THE MEATBALLS
250 g (8 oz) extra-lean minced beef
40 g (1½ oz) long-grain rice
3 tablespoons chopped parsley, plus extra to garnish (optional)
¼ teaspoon grated nutmeg

Heat the butter in a large saucepan, add the onion and fry gently for 5 minutes until just turning golden around the edges. Stir in the potato and root vegetables, the tomatoes and lemon.

Pour in the stock and lager, then add the spices and season well with salt and pepper. Bring to the boil, stirring, then cover and simmer for 45 minutes.

Meanwhile, make the meatballs. Mix all the ingredients together. Divide into 18 and shape into small balls with wetted hands. Chill until needed.

Add the meatballs to the soup, bring the soup back to the boil, then cover and simmer for 10 minutes. Add the cabbage and cook for 10 minutes until the cabbage is tender and the meatballs cooked all the way through. Taste and adjust the seasoning. Ladle into shallow bowls and sprinkle with a little chopped parsley, if liked.

VENISON, RED WINE & LENTIL SOUP

SERVES 6
PREPARATION TIME 20 minutes
COOKING TIME about 1½ hours

6 venison sausages
1 tablespoon olive oil
1 onion, roughly chopped
2 garlic cloves, finely chopped
200 g (7 oz) potatoes, diced
1 carrot, diced
4 tomatoes, skinned if liked,
    roughly chopped
125 g (4 oz) dried green lentils,
    rinsed
300 ml (½ pint) red wine

1.5 litres (2½ pints) beef stock
    (see pages 7–9)
2 tablespoons cranberry
    sauce
1 tablespoon tomato purée
1 teaspoon ground allspice
1 thyme sprig
2 bay leaves
salt and pepper
parsley, to serve

Grill the sausages until browned and just cooked. Meanwhile heat the oil in a large saucepan, add the onion and fry for 5 minutes until softened and just beginning to brown. Add the garlic, potatoes and carrot and fry briefly, then mix in the tomatoes and lentils.

Pour in the wine and stock, then add the cranberry sauce, tomato purée, allspice and herbs. Season well with salt and pepper, then slice the sausages and add these to the pan. Bring to the boil, stirring, then cover and simmer gently for 1¼ hours. Taste and adjust the seasoning if needed.

Ladle the soup into bowls and serve with croûtons tossed with a little garlic and sprinkled with parsley.

PHEASANT, BACON & BLACK PUDDING SOUP

SERVES 6
PREPARATION TIME 20 minutes
COOKING TIME about 1½ hours

1 tablespoon olive oil
1 onion, roughly chopped
150 g (5 oz) smoked streaky
  bacon, diced
2 garlic cloves, finely chopped
200 g (7 oz) potatoes, diced
1 carrot, diced
4 tomatoes, skinned if liked,
  roughly chopped
125 g (4 oz) dried green lentils,
  rinsed
125 (4 oz) black pudding,
  diced

125 g (4 oz) leftover meat from
  a roast pheasant, diced
300 ml (½ pint) red wine
1.5 litres (2½ pints) pheasant
  stock (see pages 7–9)
2 tablespoons cranberry
  sauce
1 tablespoon tomato purée
1 teaspoon ground allspice
1 thyme sprig
2 bay leaves
salt and pepper

Heat the oil in a large saucepan, add the onion and bacon, and fry for 5 minutes until softened and just beginning to brown. Add the garlic, potatoes and carrot and fry briefly, then mix in the tomatoes, lentils, black pudding and the leftover roast pheasant.

Pour in the wine and stock, then add the cranberry sauce, tomato purée, allspice and herbs. Season well with salt and pepper. Bring to the boil, stirring, then cover and simmer gently for 1¼ hours. Taste and adjust seasoning if needed.

Ladle the soup into bowls and serve with croûtons and sprinkle with chopped parsley.

HUNGARIAN CHORBA

SERVES 6
PREPARATION TIME 25 minutes
COOKING TIME 2½ hours

1 tablespoon sunflower oil

500 g (1 lb) stewing lamb on the bone

1 onion, finely chopped

1 carrot, roughly chopped

150 g (5 oz) swede, roughly chopped

2 teaspoons smoked paprika

50 g (2 oz) long-grain rice

small bunch of dill, plus extra, torn, to garnish

1.5 litres (2½ pints) lamb stock (see pages 7–9)

4–6 tablespoons red wine vinegar

2 tablespoons brown sugar

2 eggs

salt and pepper

Heat the oil in a large saucepan, add the lamb and brown on one side, turn over and add the onion, carrot and swede and cook until both sides of the lamb are browned.

Sprinkle over the paprika, cook briefly, then add the rice, dill and stock. Spoon in the vinegar, sugar and plenty of salt and pepper, then bring to the boil, stirring. Cover and simmer for 2½ hours until the lamb is very tender.

Lift the lamb out of the saucepan with a slotted spoon, transfer to a chopping board and cut the meat into small pieces, discarding the bones and fat. Return the lamb to the pan. Beat the eggs in a bowl, gradually mix in a ladleful of hot soup, then pour into the saucepan. Heat gently until the soup has thickened slightly, but do not boil or the eggs will scramble. Taste and adjust the seasoning and vinegar if needed. Garnish with dill and ladle into bowls. Serve with sliced pumpernickel bread.

LAMB & BARLEY HOTCHPOT

SERVES 6
PREPARATION TIME 20 minutes
COOKING TIME 2 hours

25 g (1 oz) butter
250 g (8 oz) lamb fillet, diced
1 large onion, finely chopped
1 leek, sliced, white and green
  parts kept separate
175 g (6 oz) swede, diced
175 g (6 oz) carrot, diced

175 g (6 oz) potato, diced
50 g (2 oz) pearl barley
2 litres (3½ pints) lamb stock
  (see pages 7–9)
2–3 rosemary sprigs, plus
  extra to serve
salt and pepper

Heat the butter in a large saucepan, add the lamb and onion and fry for 5 minutes, stirring, until the lamb is browned and the onion just beginning to colour.

Stir in the white part of the leek, the diced vegetables, pearl barley, stock and rosemary. Season with salt and pepper and bring to the boil. Cover and simmer for 1¾ hours, stirring occasionally until the meat and vegetables are very tender. Taste and adjust the seasoning if needed.

Discard the rosemary, add the green leek and cook for 10 minutes.

Ladle into bowls and sprinkle with a little chopped rosemary to serve.

CHICKEN SOUP WITH LOCKSHEN

SERVES 6
PREPARATION TIME 20 minutes
COOKING TIME 5 minutes

2 litres (3½ pints) chicken stock (see pages 7–9)
150–200 g (5–7 oz) cooked chicken, shredded
100 g (3½ oz) lockshen (vermicelli pasta)
salt and pepper
chopped parsley, to garnish (optional)

Bring the stock to the boil in a large saucepan, add the chicken and heat thoroughly. Meanwhile, bring a second pan of water to the boil, add the lockshen and simmer for 4–5 minutes until tender.

Drain the lockshen, divide it between bowls so that it makes a small nest in the base of each, then ladle the soup on top. Garnish with a little parsley, if liked.

CHICKEN & KOHLRABI CHORBA

SERVES 6
PREPARATION TIME 25 minutes
COOKING TIME 2½ hours

1 tablespoon sunflower oil
6 chicken thighs
   (about 500 g / 1 lb)
1 onion, finely chopped
1 carrot, roughly chopped
150 g (5 oz) kohlrabi, peeled
   and diced
2 teaspoons smoked paprika
50 g (2 oz) long-grain rice
small bunch of dill, plus extra,
   torn, to garnish

1.5 litres (2½ pints) lamb stock
   (see pages 7–9)
4–6 tablespoons red wine
   vinegar
2 tablespoons brown sugar
2 eggs
salt and pepper

Heat the oil in a large saucepan, fry the chicken and brown on one side, turn over and add the onion, carrot and kohlrabi and cook until both sides of the chicken are browned.

Sprinkle over the paprika, cook briefly, then add the rice, dill and stock. Spoon in the vinegar, sugar and plenty of salt and pepper, then bring to the boil, stirring. Cover and simmer for 1½ hours until the chicken is very tender.

Lift the chicken out of the saucepan with a slotted spoon, transfer to a chopping board and cut the meat into small pieces, discarding the bones and skin. Return the chicken to the pan. Beat the eggs in a bowl, gradually mix in a ladleful of hot soup, then pour into the saucepan. Heat gently until the soup has thickened slightly, but do not boil or the eggs will scramble. Taste and adjust the seasoning and vinegar if needed. Garnish with dill and ladle into bowls. Serve with sliced pumpernickel bread.

CARIBBEAN PEPPER POT SOUP

SERVES 6
PREPARATION TIME 20 minutes
COOKING TIME about 50 minutes

2 tablespoons olive oil
1 onion, finely chopped
1 Scotch bonnet chilli, deseeded and finely chopped or 2 hot Thai red chillies, chopped with seeds
2 red peppers, cored, deseeded and diced
2 garlic cloves, finely chopped
1 large carrot, diced
200 g (7 oz) potatoes, diced

1 bay leaf
1 thyme sprig
400 ml (14 fl oz) can full-fat coconut milk
600 ml (1 pint) beef stock (see pages 7–9)
salt and cayenne pepper

TO GARNISH
200 g (7 oz) rump steak
2 teaspoons olive oil

Heat the oil in a saucepan, add the onion and fry gently for 5 minutes until softened and just beginning to turn golden. Stir in the chilli, red pepper, garlic, carrot, potatoes and herbs and fry for 5 minutes, stirring.

Pour in the coconut milk and stock, then season with salt and cayenne pepper. Bring to the boil, stirring, then cover and simmer for 30 minutes, or until the vegetables are tender. Discard the herbs, then taste and adjust the seasoning if needed.

Rub the steak with the oil, then season lightly with salt and cayenne pepper. Heat a griddle or frying pan and when hot add the steak and fry for 2–5 minutes on each side, to taste. Leave to stand for 5 minutes, then slice thinly. Ladle the soup into bowls, garnish with the steak slices and serve with crusty bread.

PRAWN & SPINACH PEPPER POT SOUP

SERVES 6
PREPARATION TIME 20 minutes
COOKING TIME about 50 minutes

2 tablespoons olive oil
1 onion, finely chopped
1 Scotch bonnet chilli, deseeded and finely chopped or 2 hot Thai red chillies, chopped with seeds
2 red peppers, cored, deseeded and diced
2 garlic cloves, finely chopped
1 large carrot, diced

200 g (7 oz) potatoes, diced
1 bay leaf
1 thyme sprig
400 ml (14 fl oz) can full-fat coconut milk
600 ml (1 pint) fish stock (see pages 7–9)
200 g (7 oz) raw peeled prawns, defrosted if frozen
125 g (4 oz) spinach
salt and cayenne pepper

Heat the oil in a saucepan, add the onion and fry gently for 5 minutes until softened and just beginning to turn golden. Stir in the chilli, red peppers, garlic, carrot, potatoes and herbs and fry for 5 minutes, stirring.

Pour in the coconut milk and stock, then season with salt and cayenne pepper. Bring to the boil, stirring, then cover and simmer for 30 minutes, or until the vegetables are tender. Discard the herbs, then taste and adjust the seasoning if needed.

Add the prawns and spinach. Cook for 3–4 minutes until the prawns are pink and cooked through and the spinach is just wilted.

Ladle the soup into bowls and serve with crusty bread.

CAJUN RED BEAN SOUP

SERVES 6
PREPARATION TIME 25 minutes
COOKING TIME 1 hour

2 tablespoons sunflower oil
1 large onion, chopped
1 red pepper, diced
1 carrot, diced
1 baking potato, diced
2–3 garlic cloves, chopped
  (optional)
2 teaspoons Cajun spice
400 g (13 oz) can chopped
  tomatoes

1 tablespoon brown sugar
1 litre (1¾ pints) vegetable
  stock (see pages 7–8)
425 g (14 oz) can red kidney
  beans, drained and rinsed
50 g (2 oz) okra, sliced
50 g (2 oz) green beans,
  thinly sliced
salt and pepper

Heat the oil in a large frying pan. Add the onion and fry for 5 minutes until softened. Add the red pepper, carrot, potato and garlic, if using, and fry for 5 minutes. Stir in the Cajun spice, tomatoes, sugar, stock and plenty of salt and pepper and bring to the boil.

Add the kidney beans and mix together. Bring to the boil, then cover and simmer for 45 minutes until the vegetables are tender.

Add the okra and green beans, re-cover and cook for 5 minutes until just cooked. Serve with crusty bread.

BUTTERNUT SQUASH & ROSEMARY SOUP

SERVES 4
PREPARATION TIME 15 minutes
COOKING TIME 1¼ hours

1 butternut squash
2 tablespoons olive oil
a few rosemary sprigs, plus
   extra to garnish
150 g (5 oz) dried red lentils,
   rinsed

1 onion, finely chopped
900 ml (1½ pints) vegetable
   stock (see pages 7–9)
salt and pepper

Cut the squash in half and use a spoon to scoop out the seeds and fibrous flesh. Peel and cut the squash into small chunks and place in a roasting tin. Sprinkle over the oil and rosemary, and season well with salt and pepper. Roast in a preheated oven, 200°C (400°F), Gas Mark 6, for 45 minutes.

Meanwhile, place the lentils in a saucepan, cover with water, bring to the boil and boil rapidly for 10 minutes. Strain, then return the lentils to a clean saucepan with the onion and stock and simmer for 5 minutes. Season to taste.

Remove the squash from the oven, mash the flesh with a fork and add to the soup. Simmer for 25 minutes, and then ladle into bowls. Garnish with rosemary before serving.

POTATO, CORIANDER & CELERIAC SOUP

SERVES 4
PREPARATION TIME 15 minutes
COOKING TIME 16–21 minutes

2 tablespoons olive oil
1 onion, chopped
1 garlic clove, chopped
½ teaspoon each of ground
    cumin and coriander
pinch of chilli flakes
2 small celeriac, peeled and
    finely diced

2 potatoes, peeled and finely
    diced
1 litre (1¾ pints) vegetable
    stock (see pages 7–9)
25 g (1 oz) coriander, chopped

TO SERVE
65 g (2½ oz) crème fraîche
toasted cumin seeds

Heat the oil in a saucepan and add the onion, garlic, ground cumin and coriander and chilli flakes. Fry over a medium heat for 1 minute.

Add the celeriac and potatoes, cover with the stock and bring to the boil. Simmer for 15–20 minutes, or until the vegetables are tender.

Stir in the coriander and blend with a handheld blender until fairly smooth.

Ladle into bowls and top with a dollop of crème fraîche and toasted cumin seeds.

ROASTED ROOT VEGETABLE SOUP

SERVES 6
PREPARATION TIME 10 minutes
COOKING TIME 1 hour 5 minutes

4 carrots, chopped
2 parsnips, chopped
olive oil spray
1 leek, finely chopped
1.2 litres (2 pints) vegetable
   stock (see pages 7–9)

2 teaspoons thyme leaves
salt and pepper
thyme sprigs, to garnish

Place the carrots and parsnips in a roasting tin, spray lightly with olive oil and season with salt and pepper. Roast in a preheated oven, 200°C (400°F), Gas Mark 6, for 1 hour, or until the vegetables are very soft.

Meanwhile, 20 minutes before the vegetables have finished roasting, put the leek in a large saucepan with the stock and 1 teaspoon of the thyme. Cover the pan and simmer for 20 minutes.

Transfer the roasted root vegetables to a blender or food processor and blend, adding a little of the stock if necessary. Transfer to the stock saucepan and season to taste. Add the remaining thyme, stir and simmer for 5 minutes to reheat.

Ladle into bowls and serve garnished with thyme sprigs.

HONEY-ROASTED PARSNIP SOUP

SERVES 6
PREPARATION TIME 20 minutes
COOKING TIME 50–55 minutes

750 g (1½ lb) parsnips, cut
    into wedges
2 onions, cut into wedges
2 tablespoons olive oil
2 tablespoons clear honey
1 teaspoon ground turmeric
½ teaspoon dried crushed
    chillies
3 garlic cloves, thickly sliced
1.2 litres (2 pints) vegetable
    or chicken stock
    (see pages 7–9)

2 tablespoons sherry vinegar
    or cider vinegar
150 ml (¼ pint) double cream
5 cm (2 inch) piece root ginger,
    peeled and grated
salt and pepper

TO SERVE
a little turmeric (optional)
croûtons

Arrange the parsnips and onions in a large roasting tin in a single layer, then drizzle with the oil and honey. Sprinkle with the turmeric, chillies and garlic.

Roast in a preheated oven, 190°C (375°F), Gas Mark 5, for 45–50 minutes, turning once until the vegetables are a deep golden brown with sticky, caramelized edges.

Transfer the roasting tin to the hob, add the stock, vinegar and season with salt and pepper. Bring to the boil, scraping up the juices from the base of the pan. Simmer for 5 minutes.

Allow the soup to cool slightly, then purée in batches in a blender or food processor until smooth. Pour into a saucepan and reheat. Taste and adjust the seasoning and top up with a little extra stock, if needed. Mix the cream, ginger and a little pepper together. Ladle the soup into bowls and drizzle the ginger cream over the top, then garnish with a little turmeric, if liked. Serve with croûtons.

INDIAN SPICED BUTTERNUT SQUASH SOUP

SERVES 4
PREPARATION TIME 15 minutes
COOKING TIME 1¼ hours

1 butternut squash
2 tablespoons olive oil
a few rosemary sprigs, plus
    extra to garnish
150 g (5 oz) dried red lentils,
    rinsed
1 tablespoon sunflower oil
1 onion, finely chopped

2 teaspoons mild curry paste
3.5 cm (1½ inch) piece root
    ginger, finely chopped
900 ml (1½ pints) vegetable
    stock (see pages 7–9)
salt and pepper
torn coriander leaves,
    to garnish

Cut the squash in half and use a spoon to scoop out the seeds and fibrous flesh. Peel and cut the squash into small chunks and place in a roasting tin. Sprinkle over the olive oil and rosemary, and season well with salt and pepper. Roast in a preheated oven, 200°C (400°F), Gas Mark 6, for 45 minutes.

Meanwhile, place the lentils in a saucepan, cover with water, bring to the boil and boil rapidly for 10 minutes. Strain and set aside.

Heat the sunflower oil in a saucepan, add the onion and fry for 5 minutes until softened. Stir in curry paste, ginger and the drained lentils and stock, and simmer for 5 minutes.

Remove the squash from the oven, mash the flesh with a fork and add to the soup. Simmer for 25 minutes, and then ladle into bowls. Garnish with the coriander before serving.

ROASTED CAULIFLOWER SOUP WITH CRUNCHY LEAF CROÛTONS

SERVES 4
PREPARATION TIME 10 minutes
COOKING TIME about 40 minutes

1 cauliflower, cut into small
   florets, leaves reserved
4 tablespoons olive oil
1 onion, roughly chopped
leaves from 2 thyme sprigs

4 garlic cloves, finely grated
1.5 litres (2½ pints) vegetable
   stock (see pages 7–9)
juice of ½ lemon
salt and pepper

Place the cauliflower florets on a baking tray and toss with 2 tablespoons of the oil. Season well and roast in a preheat the oven to 200°C (400°F), Gas Mark 6, for 20 minutes.

Meanwhile, in a large saucepan, cook the onion with 1 tablespoon of the oil until translucent and soft. Add the thyme leaves and garlic and cook for 1 minute until fragrant. Pour in the stock and bring to a simmer.

When the cauliflower florets are browned, toss the cauliflower leaves with the remaining 1 tablespoon of oil, season with salt and pepper and roast for 5–10 minutes until crisp. Meanwhile, add the florets to the pan of stock and cook for 5 minutes.

Use a stick blender to whizz the soup until smooth. Stir in the lemon juice, taste and adjust the seasoning if needed. Serve with the crispy cauliflower leaf croûtons.

CREAM OF LEEK & PEA SOUP

SERVES 6
PREPARATION TIME 15 minutes
COOKING TIME 20 minutes

2 tablespoons olive oil
375 g (12 oz) leeks, slit and well washed, then thinly sliced
375 g (12 oz) fresh shelled or frozen peas
900 ml (1½ pints) vegetable or chicken stock (see pages 7–9)
small bunch of mint

150 g (5 oz) full-fat mascarpone
grated rind of 1 small lemon
salt and pepper

TO GARNISH
mint leaves (optional)
lemon rind curls (optional)

Heat the oil in a saucepan, add the leeks and fry gently for 10 minutes, covered and stirring occasionally, until softened but not coloured. Mix in the peas and cook briefly.

Pour the stock into the pan, add a little salt and pepper, then bring to the boil. Cover and simmer gently for 10 minutes.

Ladle half the soup into a blender or food processor, add the mint and blend until smooth. Pour the purée back into the saucepan. In a small bowl, mix the mascarpone with half the lemon rind, reserving the rest for garnishing.

Spoon half the mixture into the soup, then reheat, stirring until the mascarpone has melted. Taste and adjust the seasoning if needed. Ladle the soup into bowls, top with spoonfuls of the remaining mascarpone and a sprinkling of the remaining lemon rind. Garnish with mint leaves and lemon rind curls, if liked.

PESTO, PEA & BROCCOLI SOUP

SERVES 4
PREPARATION TIME 5 minutes
COOKING TIME 25 minutes

2 tablespoons olive oil
1 onion, finely chopped
1 baking potato
   (about 275 g / 9 oz), diced
1 garlic clove, chopped
200 g (7 oz) can chopped
   tomatoes
900 ml (1½ pints) vegetable
   stock (see pages 7–9)

175 g (6 oz) broccoli, cut into
   small florets and stalks
   sliced
125 g (4 oz) frozen peas
2 teaspoons green pesto, plus
   extra to garnish
salt and pepper
a few basil leaves, to garnish
grated Parmesan, to serve

Heat the oil in a large saucepan, add the onion and fry for 5 minutes until lightly browned. Add the potato and garlic and fry for 5 minutes, stirring, until softened.

Add the tomatoes and stock, and season with salt and pepper, then bring to the boil. Cover the pan and simmer for 10 minutes until reduced and thickened. Add the broccoli, peas and pesto and simmer for 3–4 minutes until the broccoli is just tender.

Garnish the soup with a little extra pesto and the basil and serve with Parmesan.

RED PEPPER & CARROT SOUP

SERVES 4
PREPARATION TIME 15 minutes
COOKING TIME about 40 minutes

2 tablespoons olive oil
2 onions, finely chopped
1 garlic clove, crushed
3 red peppers, cored,
  deseeded and roughly
  chopped
2 carrots, diced

900 ml (1½ pints) vegetable
  stock (see pages 7–9)
salt and pepper

TO SERVE
8 teaspoonfuls garlic and herb
  soft cheese
chives, chopped

Heat the oil in a large saucepan and fry the onions gently for 5 minutes, or until softened and golden brown. Add the garlic and cook gently for 1 minute. Add the peppers and carrots and fry for 5–8 minutes, or until softened.

Add the stock to the pan, season to taste with salt and pepper and bring to the boil. Reduce the heat, cover and simmer gently for 20 minutes.

Allow the soup to cool slightly once the vegetables are tender, then purée in batches in a blender or food processor. Return the soup to the pan, reheat and adjust the seasoning if needed. Serve topped with soft cheese and some chives.

SPINACH & RED LENTIL SOUP

SERVES 4
PREPARATION TIME 10 minutes
COOKING TIME 15 minutes

250 g (8 oz) dried red lentils, rinsed

900 ml (1½ pints) cold water

3 tablespoons sunflower oil

1 large onion, finely chopped

2 garlic cloves, crushed

2.5 cm (1 inch) piece root ginger, peeled and grated

1 red chilli, deseeded and chopped, plus extra to garnish (optional)

1 tablespoon medium curry powder

300 ml (½ pint) vegetable stock (see pages 7–9)

200 g (7 oz) canned chopped tomatoes

100 g (3½ oz) baby spinach

25 g (1 oz) coriander leaves, chopped, plus extra to garnish

100 ml (3½ fl oz) coconut cream

salt and pepper

65 g (2½ oz) natural yogurt, to serve

Put the lentils into a medium saucepan and cover with the measured water. Bring to the boil, skimming off the scum as it rises to the surface, and simmer for 10 minutes until the lentils are tender and just falling apart. Remove from the heat, cover and set aside.

Meanwhile, heat the oil in a large saucepan, add the onion and fry gently for 5 minutes. Add the garlic, ginger and chilli and fry for a further 2 minutes. Stir in the curry powder and ½ teaspoon black pepper and cook for a further 2 minutes.

Add the stock, the lentils and their cooking liquid, the tomatoes, spinach and coriander and season with salt to taste. Cover and simmer for 5 minutes, then add the coconut cream.

Whizz the mixture with a hand-held blender until the soup is almost smooth.

Ladle the soup into bowls, swirl each with a spoonful of yogurt and garnish with coriander leaves, freshly ground black pepper and finely chopped red chilli, if desired.

CHICKPEA SOUP WITH DUMPLINGS

SERVES 4
PREPARATION TIME 20 minutes
COOKING TIME 30 minutes

2 tablespoons olive oil
1 onion, finely chopped
1 carrot, peeled and finely chopped
2 celery sticks, finely chopped
3 garlic cloves, crushed
1 teaspoon ground cumin
½ teaspoon ground turmeric
2 bay leaves
750 ml (1¼ pints) vegetable stock (see pages 7–9)
400 g (13 oz) can chickpeas, drained and rinsed
finely grated zest and juice of 1 lemon
½ teaspoon celery salt (or regular salt)
salt and pepper
4 tablespoons roughly chopped celery leaves, to serve

FOR THE DUMPLINGS
200 g (7 oz) gram flour
1 teaspoon baking powder
½ teaspoon celery salt (or regular salt)
½ teaspoon ground black pepper
100 ml (3½ fl oz) oat milk
100 ml (3½ fl oz) water

Heat the oil in a medium saucepan, add the onion, carrot, celery and garlic and cook over a medium heat for about 8 minutes until soft, stirring often so that the vegetables do not colour too much.

Stir in the spices and cook for another 2 minutes. Add all the remaining soup ingredients, except the celery leaves, stir to combine, and season with salt and pepper to taste. Bring to a gentle simmer and cook for about 10 minutes.

Meanwhile, make the dumplings. Mix all the dry ingredients together in a bowl. Make a well in the centre. Whisk together the oat milk and the measured water in a jug, then mix into the dumpling mixture until you have a thick batter.

Dollop tablespoons of the dumpling batter onto the surface of the soup, leaving a little space in between – it should make about 8–10 dumplings. Cover with the lid and cook for 8 minutes until the dumplings are fluffy but firm.

Serve the soup and dumplings in bowls with the celery leaves scattered over.

HOT & SOUR NOODLE SOUP

SERVES 4
PREPARATION TIME 15 minutes
COOKING TIME 35–40 minutes

2 tablespoons sesame oil
2 garlic cloves, finely sliced
2 cm (¾ inch) piece root ginger, peeled and grated
150 g (5 oz) shiitake mushrooms, sliced
100 g (3½ oz) oyster mushrooms, sliced
2 red chillies, deseeded and finely chopped
1.5 litres (2½ pints) vegetable stock (see pages 7–9)
3 tablespoons light soy sauce
4 teaspoons rice wine vinegar
1½ tablespoons Chinese Shaoxing rice wine or dry sherry

1½ tablespoons light brown sugar
½ teaspoon ground black pepper
100 g (3½ oz) canned sliced bamboo shoots, drained
100 g (3½ oz) rice, ramen or soba noodles
3 tablespoons cornflour
3 tablespoons water
salt, if needed

TO SERVE
3 spring onions, finely sliced
lime wedges

Heat the oil in a large saucepan, add the garlic and ginger and cook over a medium heat for 4 minutes. Add the mushrooms and chillies and cook for about 10 minutes until the mushrooms are softened and caramelized.

Pour over the stock, soy sauce, vinegar and rice wine or sherry and sprinkle in the sugar and pepper, then simmer for 20 minutes to allow the flavours to mingle.

Stir in the bamboo shoots and cook the noodles according to the packet instructions.

Just before the noodles are ready, mix the cornflour with the measured water until smooth, add to the soup and cook, stirring, for about 2 minutes until thickened. Taste and add salt if needed.

Serve in bowls topped with the spring onions and some lime wedges on the side.

SOMETHING DIFFERENT

BLOODY MARY SOUP

SERVES 6
PREPARATION TIME 20 minutes
COOKING TIME 25 minutes + chilling

1 tablespoon olive oil,
  plus extra to serve
1 onion, chopped
1 red pepper, cored, deseeded
  and diced
2 celery sticks, sliced
500 g (1 lb) plum tomatoes,
  chopped
900 ml (1½ pints) vegetable
  stock (see pages 7–9)

2 teaspoons caster sugar
4 teaspoons Worcestershire
  sauce
4 teaspoons tomato purée
4 tablespoons vodka
a few drops of Tabasco sauce
salt and pepper
6 baby celery sticks with
  leaves, to garnish

Heat the oil in a saucepan, add the onion and fry until softened but not browned. Stir in the pepper, celery and tomatoes and fry for 5 minutes.

Pour in the stock, add the sugar, Worcestershire sauce, tomato purée, a little salt and pepper and bring to the boil. Cover and simmer for 15 minutes.

Allow the soup to cool, then purée in a blender or food processor. Pour back into the saucepan. Add the vodka and Tabasco to taste, and adjust the seasoning if needed. Chill well.

Ladle the soup into small bowls, add a celery stick, drizzle with olive oil and sprinkle with a little extra pepper.

GAZPACHO

SERVES 6
PREPARATION TIME 10–15 minutes + chilling

2 garlic cloves, roughly
  chopped
¼ teaspoon salt
3 slices of thick white bread,
  crusts removed
375 g (12 oz) tomatoes,
  skinned and coarsely
  chopped
½ large cucumber, peeled,
  deseeded and coarsely
  chopped
1 large red pepper, cored,
  deseeded and coarsely
  chopped

2 celery sticks, quartered
5 tablespoons olive oil
4 tablespoons white wine
  vinegar
1 litre (1¾ pints) water
freshly ground black pepper

TO GARNISH
2 tomatoes, deseeded
  and diced
¼ cucumber, diced
½ red onion, finely chopped

Combine the garlic and salt in a mortar and pound with a pestle until smooth. Alternatively, place the garlic and salt on a board and crush the garlic with the flattened blade of a knife. Place the bread in a bowl and cover with cold water. Soak for 5 seconds, then drain the bread and squeeze out the moisture.

Place the tomatoes, cucumber, pepper and celery in a blender or food processor. Add the garlic paste, bread and oil and purée the mixture until very smooth.

Pour the mixture into a large bowl and stir in the vinegar and measured water and season with pepper to taste. Cover with clingfilm and chill in the refrigerator for at least 3 hours. Serve the soup very cold in chilled glasses. Garnish with a sprinkling of diced tomatoes, cucumber and red onion.

CHEAT'S CURRIED VEGETABLE SOUP

SERVES 6
PREPARATION TIME 25 minutes
COOKING TIME 40 minutes

2 tablespoons sunflower oil
1 onion, finely chopped
2 garlic cloves, finely chopped
4 teaspoons mild curry paste
2.5 cm (1 inch) piece root ginger, peeled and grated
2 small baking potatoes, diced
2 carrots, diced
1 small cauliflower, core discarded, florets cut into small pieces
75 g (3 oz) dried red lentils, rinsed
1.5 litres (2½ pints) vegetable (see pages 7–9)

400 g (13 oz) can chopped tomatoes
200 g (7 oz) spinach leaves, rinsed and any large leaves torn into pieces
salt and pepper

FOR THE RAITA
150 g (5 oz) low-fat natural yogurt
4 tablespoons chopped coriander leaves
4 teaspoons mango chutney

Heat the oil in a large saucepan, add the onion and fry for 5 minutes, stirring until softened. Stir in the garlic, curry paste and ginger and cook for 1 minute.

Mix in the potatoes, carrots, cauliflower and lentils. Pour in the stock and tomatoes, season with salt and pepper and bring to the boil. Cover and simmer for 30 minutes, or until the lentils are tender.

Meanwhile, make the raita. Mix the yogurt, coriander and mango chutney together in a small bowl.

Add the spinach to the soup and cook for 2 minutes until just wilted. Taste and adjust the seasoning if needed. Ladle the soup into shallow bowls and top with spoonfuls of raita. Serve with warmed naan breads, if liked.

FENNEL & TROUT SOUP

SERVES 4
PREPARATION TIME 20 minutes
COOKING TIME about 25 minutes

50 ml (2 fl oz) olive oil
3 large spring onions, chopped
250 g (8 oz) fennel bulb, trimmed, cored and finely sliced
1 potato, peeled and diced

finely grated rind and juice of 1 lemon
900 ml (1½ pints) chicken or vegetable stock (see pages 7–9)
2 boneless trout fillets
salt and pepper

Heat the oil in a large saucepan and fry the spring onions for 5 minutes until soft. Add the fennel, potato and lemon rind and cook for 5 minutes until the fennel begins to soften. Pour in the stock and bring to the boil. Reduce the heat, cover the pan and simmer for about 15 minutes until the ingredients are tender. Taste and season well with salt and pepper and lemon juice

Meanwhile, steam the trout fillets above the simmering soup for 10 minutes, until the fish flakes easily when pressed with a knife. Lift the trout out of the steamer, remove the skin, then break into flakes, removing any bones.

Spoon the fish into bowls, then ladle the soup over the top. Serve with slices of crusty bread.

BACON &
EGG-DROP MISO

SERVES 2
PREPARATION TIME 10 minutes
COOKING TIME about 10 minutes

2 slices of streaky bacon, chopped into small pieces

2 spring onions, thinly sliced

2 teaspoons brown miso paste

500 ml (17 fl oz) just-boiled water

½ teaspoon grated fresh turmeric or ground turmeric

2 large handfuls of baby spinach

2 eggs, beaten

Heat a nonstick saucepan and fry the bacon over a medium heat, adding the spring onions after a couple of minutes.

Dissolve the miso paste in a little just-boiled water and add to the pan, along with the rest of the just-boiled measured water and the turmeric. Allow the flavours to infuse for a couple of minutes before adding the spinach.

When the spinach has wilted down a little, slowly add the beaten eggs to the soup, ideally through a slotted spoon to help create ribbons.

As soon as the egg sets, remove from the heat, divide between bowls and serve.

GHANAIAN GROUNDNUT SOUP WITH FOO FOO

SERVES 6
PREPARATION TIME 15 minutes
COOKING TIME about 40 minutes

1 tablespoon sunflower oil
1 onion, finely chopped
2 carrots, diced
500 g (1 lb) tomatoes, skinned
    if liked, roughly chopped
½ teaspoon piri piri seasoning
    or crushed chilli flakes
100 g (3½ oz) roasted salted
    peanuts
1 litre (1¾ pints) fish or
    vegetable stock
    (see pages 7–9)

FOR THE FOO FOO
750 g (1½ lb) yam or cassava,
    cut into chunks
3 tablespoons milk
salt and pepper

TO GARNISH
crushed chilli flakes
peanuts, roughly chopped

Heat the oil in a saucepan, add the onion and carrots and fry for 5 minutes, stirring until softened and just turning golden around the edges. Stir in the tomatoes and piri piri and cook for 1 minute.

Grind the peanuts to a fine powder in a spice mill or food processor. Stir into the pan, add the stock and bring to the boil. Cover and simmer for 30 minutes.

Make the foo foo. Cook the yam or cassava in a saucepan of boiling water for 20 minutes until tender. Drain and mash with the milk and seasoning. Shape into 6 balls and set aside.

Mash or purée half the soup and reheat. Taste and adjust the seasoning if needed, then ladle into bowls, garnish with crushed chilli flakes and peanuts and serve with the foo foo on the side for dunking into the hot soup.

MUSHROOM & MADEIRA SOUP

SERVES 6
PREPARATION TIME 30 minutes
COOKING TIME 40 minutes

50 g (2 oz) butter
1 tablespoon olive oil
1 onion, chopped
400 g (13 oz) cup mushrooms,
  sliced
2 large flat mushrooms, sliced
2 garlic cloves, finely chopped
125 ml (4 fl oz) Madeira or
  medium sherry
900 ml (1½ pints) chicken
  or vegetable stock
  (see pages 7–9)

40 g (1½ oz) long-grain rice
2 thyme sprigs
450 ml (¾ pint) milk
150 ml (¼ pint) double cream
salt and pepper

TO GARNISH
25 g (1 oz) butter
250 g (8 oz) exotic
  mushrooms
few extra thyme leaves

Heat the butter and oil in a large saucepan, add the onion and fry gently for 5 minutes until just turning golden around the edges. Add the mushrooms and garlic and fry over a high heat for 2–3 minutes until golden.

Stir in the Madeira, stock, rice and thyme, then season with salt and pepper and bring to the boil. Cover and simmer for 30 minutes.

Allow the soup to cool slightly and discard the thyme sprigs. Purée the soup in batches in a blender or food processor until smooth. Return to the saucepan and stir in the milk and cream. Reheat without boiling, then taste and adjust the seasoning if needed.

Make the garnish. Heat the butter in a frying pan and slice any large mushrooms, then fry for 2 minutes until golden. Ladle the soup into shallow bowls and gently spoon the mushrooms into the centre. Garnish with a few thyme leaves and serve with savoury scones.

PUMPKIN, ORANGE & STAR ANISE SOUP WITH SPICED ORANGE & CHILLI BUTTER

SERVES 6
PREPARATION TIME 25 minutes
COOKING TIME 50 minutes

25 g (1 oz) butter
1 onion, roughly chopped
1 pumpkin (about 1.5 kg / 3 lb),
  quartered, deseeded,
  peeled and diced
zest and juice of
  2 small oranges
1 litre (1¾ pints) vegetable
  or chicken stock
  (see pages 7–9)
3 whole star anise or similar
  amount in pieces, plus
  extra to garnish

salt and pepper
crushed black peppercorns,
  to garnish (optional)

FOR THE SPICED ORANGE & CHILLI BUTTER
75 g (3 oz) butter
grated rind of 1 orange
1 large mild red chilli,
  deseeded and finely
  chopped
pinch of ground turmeric
pinch of ground cloves

Heat the butter in a large saucepan, add the onion and fry gently for 5 minutes until softened. Add the pumpkin, toss in the butter and fry for 5 minutes, stirring.

Mix in the orange rind and juice, the stock and star anise. Season with salt and pepper and bring to the boil. Cover and simmer for 30 minutes, stirring occasionally until the pumpkin is soft. Scoop out the star anise and reserve.

Allow the soup to cool slightly, then purée in batches in a blender or food processor until smooth. Pour back into the saucepan and reheat. Taste and adjust the seasoning if needed.

Make the spiced orange and chilli butter. Beat the butter with the orange rind, chilli and spices. Shape into a sausage then wrap in clingfilm to chill.

Ladle the soup into bowls and garnish each bowl with a whole star anise and a sprinkling of black pepper. Unwrap the spiced orange and chilli butter, slice and add a slice to each portion of soup. Serve with sesame bread rolls.

SEAFOOD GUMBO

SERVES 6
PREPARATION TIME 20 minutes
COOKING TIME 30 minutes

1 tablespoon sunflower oil
1 onion, finely chopped
1 small carrot, diced
1 celery stick, diced
½ red pepper, cored, deseeded and diced
425 g (14 oz) tomatoes, skinned if liked, roughly chopped
large thyme sprig
¼ teaspoon crushed chilli flakes
2 teaspoons tomato purée
1 litre (1¾ pints) vegetable or fish stock (see pages 7–9)
40 g (1½ oz) long-grain rice
400 g (13 oz) frozen seafood selection, defrosted, rinsed with cold water and drained
43 g (1½ oz) can dressed crab
75 g (3 oz) okra, trimmed, sliced
salt and pepper
a few extra thyme leaves, to garnish (optional)

Heat the oil in a saucepan, add the onion and fry gently for 5 minutes until softened and just beginning to brown. Stir in the carrot, celery and red pepper and fry for a few more minutes. Mix in the tomatoes, thyme, chilli and tomato purée, then pour in the stock. Add the rice, season with salt and pepper and bring to the boil.

Cover and simmer for 20 minutes, stirring occasionally. Halve any very large mussels, then stir into the soup with the remaining seafood, canned crab and okra. Cover and simmer for 5 minutes, then taste and adjust the seasoning if needed. Ladle into bowls and sprinkle with a few thyme leaves, if liked. Serve with crusty bread.

SMOOTH CARROT SOUP WITH MINT OIL

SERVES 6
PREPARATION TIME 20 minutes
COOKING TIME 1–1¼ hours

2 tablespoons olive oil
1 onion, roughly chopped
750 g (1½ lb) carrots, diced
40 g (1½ oz) long-grain rice
1 litre (1¾ pints) vegetable
　or chicken stock
　(see pages 7–9)
300 ml (½ pint) milk
salt and pepper

FOR THE MINT OIL
15 g (½ oz) fresh mint, plus
　extra to garnish
¼ teaspoon caster sugar
3 tablespoons olive oil

Heat the oil in a saucepan, add the onion and fry for
5 minutes until just beginning to soften and turn golden
around the edges. Stir in the carrots and cook for 5 minutes.
Mix in the rice, stock and a little salt and pepper. Bring to
the boil, then cover and simmer for 45 minutes, stirring
occasionally until the carrots are tender.

Meanwhile, make the mint oil. Strip the leaves from the
mint stems and add the leaves to a blender or food processor
with the sugar and a little pepper. Finely chop, then blend in
the oil a little at a time with the motor running. Spoon into a
small bowl and stir before using.

Rinse the blender or food processor, then purée the soup
in batches until smooth. Return the soup to the saucepan
and stir in the milk. Reheat, then taste and adjust the
seasoning if needed. Ladle into bowls and drizzle with the
mint oil and add some extra mint leaves, if liked. Serve with
toasted muffins.

TOMATO SOUP WITH CRISPY CHORIZO

SERVES 6
PREPARATION TIME 15 minutes
COOKING TIME about 40 minutes

2 tablespoons olive oil
1 onion, roughly chopped
2 garlic cloves, crushed
2 kg (4 lb) ripe tomatoes,
  skinned and chopped
2 tablespoons tomato
  purée
450 ml (¾ pint) vegetable or
  chicken stock, plus extra if
  needed (see pages 7–9)
75 ml (3 fl oz) red wine

4 basil sprigs
1–2 teaspoons brown sugar
salt and pepper

TO GARNISH
40 g (1½ oz) sliced chorizo
2–3 tablespoons finely
  chopped basil
150 ml (¼ pint) Greek yogurt
6 small basil sprigs

Heat the oil in a large saucepan and fry the onion and garlic until softened. Add the tomatoes, tomato purée, stock, red wine and basil. Bring to the boil, then reduce the heat, cover the pan and simmer gently for 20–25 minutes until the vegetables are soft.

Allow the soup to cool slightly, then purée in batches in a blender or food processor and push through a nylon sieve into the rinsed pan to remove the tomato seeds. Season with salt, pepper and a little sugar, to taste. Return the pan to the heat and bring to the boil, then add a little extra stock if necessary to achieve the desired consistency.

Dry-fry the chorizo until browned, then dice and set aside. Fold the basil into the Greek yogurt. Pour the hot soup into warmed bowls, spoon over a little basil yogurt and sprinkle with the crispy chorizo. Garnish with small basil sprigs.

FIVE-SPICE DUCK SOUP & PAK CHOI

SERVES 4
PREPARATION TIME 15 minutes
COOKING TIME 20 minutes

1.2 litres (2 pints) duck stock (see pages 7–9)

grated rind and juice of 1 orange

4 tablespoons medium sherry

¼ teaspoon five spice powder

5 cm (2 inch) piece root ginger, peeled and thinly sliced

1 tablespoon soy sauce

2 tablespoons Chinese plum sauce

125–175 g (4–6 oz) leftover cooked duck, stripped from carcass before stock was made

½ bunch of spring onions, thinly sliced

2 pak choi, thickly sliced

salt and pepper (optional)

Pour the stock into a saucepan, then add the orange rind and juice, sherry, five spice powder and ginger. Stir in the soy sauce and plum sauce, then bring to the boil, stirring. Cover and simmer gently for 15 minutes.

Add the duck, spring onions and pak choi and simmer for 5 minutes. Taste and add a little salt and pepper if needed, then ladle into bowls.

HERBED DUCK BROTH WITH NOODLES

SERVES 4
PREPARATION TIME 15 minutes
COOKING TIME 20 minutes

50 g (2 oz) fine dried egg
   noodles
1.2 litres (2 pints) duck stock
   (see pages 7–9)
grated rind and juice of
   ½ lemon
5 cm (2 inch) piece root ginger,
   peeled and thinly sliced
1 tablespoon soy sauce
3 tablespoons chopped
   parsley

3 tablespoons chopped mint
125–175 g (4–6 oz) leftover
   cooked duck, stripped
   from carcass before stock
   was made
½ bunch of spring onions,
   thinly sliced
2 pak choi, thickly sliced
salt and pepper (optional)

Soak the noodles in boiling water for 5 minutes.

Pour the stock into a saucepan, then add the lemon rind and juice, ginger and soy sauce and bring to the boil, stirring. Cover and simmer gently for 15 minutes.

Add the herbs, duck, spring onions and pak choi and simmer for 5 minutes. Taste and add a little salt and pepper if needed. Divide the noodles between the bowls and ladle the broth over the top.

FRAGRANT TOFU & NOODLE SOUP

SERVES 2
PREPARATION TIME 15 minutes + 10 minutes draining
COOKING TIME 10 minutes

125 g (4 oz) firm tofu, diced
1 tablespoon sesame oil
75 g (3 oz) thin dried rice noodles
600 ml (1 pint) vegetable stock (see pages 7–9)
2.5 cm (1 inch) piece root ginger, peeled and thickly sliced
1 large garlic clove, thickly sliced
3 dried kaffir lime leaves, torn in half

2 lemongrass stalks, halved and lightly bruised
handful of spinach or pak choi leaves
50 g (2 oz) beansprouts, rinsed
1–2 fresh red chillies, deseeded and finely sliced
2 tablespoons chopped coriander leaves
1 tablespoon Thai fish sauce

TO SERVE
lime wedges
chilli sauce

Put the tofu on a plate lined with kitchen paper and allow to stand for 10 minutes to drain.

Heat the oil in a wok until hot and fry the tofu for 2–3 minutes until golden brown, stirring frequently.

Meanwhile, soak the noodles in boiling water for 2 minutes, then drain.

Pour the stock into a large saucepan. Add the ginger, garlic, lime leaves and lemongrass and bring to the boil. Reduce the heat, add the tofu, noodles, spinach or pak choi, beansprouts and chillies and heat through. Add the coriander and fish sauce, then pour into deep bowls. Serve with lime wedges and chilli sauce.

THAI PRAWN BROTH

SERVES 4
PREPARATION TIME 15 minutes
COOKING TIME about 10 minutes

1.2 litres (2 pints) vegetable
  stock (see pages 7–9)
2 teaspoons ready-made
  Thai red curry paste
4 dried kaffir lime leaves,
  torn in half
3–4 teaspoons Thai fish sauce
2 spring onions, sliced
150 g (5 oz) shiitake
  mushrooms, sliced

125 g (4 oz) dried soba noodles
½ red pepper, cored, deseeded
  and diced
125 g (4 oz) pak choi, thinly
  sliced
250 g (8 oz) frozen prawns,
  defrosted and rinsed
small bunch of coriander
  leaves, torn into pieces

Pour the stock into a saucepan, add the curry paste, lime leaves, fish sauce to taste, spring onions and mushrooms. Bring to the boil and simmer for 5 minutes.

Bring a separate pan of water to the boil, add the noodles and cook for 3 minutes.

Add the remaining ingredients to the soup and cook for 2 minutes until piping hot.

Drain the noodles, rinse with fresh hot water and divide the noodles between the bowls. Ladle the hot prawn broth over the top and serve immediately.

THAI TAMARIND BROTH

SERVES 4
PREPARATION TIME 15 minutes
COOKING TIME about 10 minutes

1.2 litres (2 pints) vegetable stock (see pages 7–9)

2 teaspoons tamarind concentrate

¼ teaspoon turmeric

2 teaspoons ready-made Thai red curry paste

4 dried kaffir lime leaves, torn in half

3–4 teaspoons Thai fish sauce

2 spring onions, sliced

150 g (5 oz) shiitake mushrooms, sliced

125 g (4 oz) dried soba noodles

½ red pepper, cored, deseeded and diced

125 g (4 oz) pak choi, thinly sliced

small bunch of coriander leaves, torn

Pour the stock into a saucepan, add the tamarind, turmeric, curry paste, lime leaves, fish sauce to taste, spring onions and mushrooms. Bring to the boil and simmer for 5 minutes.

Bring a separate pan of water to the boil, add the noodles and cook for 3 minutes.

Add the remaining ingredients to the soup and cook for 2 minutes until piping hot.

Drain the noodles, rinse with fresh hot water and divide the noodles between the bowls. Ladle the hot broth over the top and serve immediately.

TOFU & SATAY SOUP

SERVES 2
PREPARATION TIME 15 minutes + 10 minutes draining
COOKING TIME 10 minutes

125 g (4 oz) firm tofu, diced
1 tablespoon sesame oil
75 g (3 oz) thin dried rice
   noodles
600 ml (1 pint) vegetable
   stock (see pages 7–9)
2.5 cm (1 inch) piece root
   ginger, peeled and
   thickly sliced
1 large garlic clove, thickly
   sliced

2 tablespoons crunchy
   peanut butter
1 tablespoon soy sauce
handful of spinach or pak
   choi leaves
50 g (2 oz) beansprouts
1–2 fresh red chillies,
   deseeded and finely sliced

TO SERVE
coriander
lime wedges

Put the tofu on a plate lined with kitchen paper and allow to stand for 10 minutes to drain.

Heat the oil in a wok until hot and fry the tofu for 2–3 minutes until golden brown, stirring frequently.

Meanwhile, soak the noodles in boiling water for 2 minutes, then drain.

Pour the stock into a large saucepan. Add the ginger and garlic, and bring to the boil. Reduce the heat, stir in the peanut butter and soy sauce. Simmer for 3 minutes, then add the tofu, noodles, spinach or pak choi, beansprouts and chillies and heat through.

Pour into deep bowls, and serve with coriander and lime wedges.

VIETNAMESE BEEF PHO

SERVES 6
PREPARATION TIME 15 minutes
COOKING TIME about 45 minutes

1 teaspoon sunflower oil
1 teaspoon Szechuan peppercorns, roughly crushed
1 lemongrass stalk, sliced
1 cinnamon stick, broken into pieces
2 star anise
4 cm (1½ inch) piece of root ginger, peeled and sliced
small bunch of coriander
1.5 litres (2½ pints) beef stock

(see pages 7–9)
1 tablespoon fish sauce
juice of 1 lime
100 g (3½ oz) fine rice noodles
250 g (8 oz) rump or flash-fry beef steak, fat trimmed, meat thinly sliced
100 g (3½ oz) beansprouts, rinsed
4 spring onions, thinly sliced
1 large mild red chilli, thinly sliced

Heat the oil in a large saucepan, add the peppercorns, lemongrass, cinnamon, star anise and ginger and cook for 1 minute to release their flavours. Cut the stems from the coriander and add the stems to the pan with the stock. Bring to the boil, stirring, then cover and simmer for 40 minutes.

Strain the stock and return to the pan. Stir in the fish sauce and lime juice. Blanch the noodles in a separate pan of boiling water for 2 minutes to soften, then drain and divide between bowls. Add the steak to the soup and cook for 1–2 minutes. Divide the beansprouts, spring onions and chilli between the bowls, then ladle the soup on top and finish with the coriander leaves, torn into pieces.

VIETNAMESE PRAWN SOUP

SERVES 6
PREPARATION TIME 15 minutes
COOKING TIME about 45 minutes

1 teaspoon sunflower oil
1 teaspoon Szechuan
    peppercorns, roughly
    crushed
1 lemo grass stalk, sliced
2 kaffir lime leaves
2 star anise
4 cm (1½ inch) piece root
    ginger, peeled and sliced
small bunch of coriander
1.5 litres (2½ pints) chicken
    or vegetable stock
    (see pages 7–9)

1 tablespoon fish sauce
juice of 1 lime
100 g (3½ oz) fine rice noodles
200 g (7 oz) raw peeled
    prawns
150 g (5 oz) button
    mushrooms, sliced
100 g (3½ oz) beansprouts,
    rinsed
4 spring onions, thinly sliced
1 large mild red chilli, thinly
    sliced

Heat the oil in a saucepan, add the peppercorns, lemongrass, kaffir lime leaves, star anise and ginger and cook for 1 minute to release their flavours. Cut the stems from the coriander and add the stems to the pan with the stock. Bring to the boil, stirring, then cover and simmer for 40 minutes.

Strain the stock and return to the pan. Stir in the fish sauce and lime juice. Blanch the noodles in a separate pan of boiling water for 2 minutes to soften, then drain and divide between bowls. Add the prawns and mushrooms to the soup and cook 4–5 minutes until the prawns are pink. Divide the beansprouts, spring onions and chilli between the bowls, then ladle the soup on top and finish with the coriander leaves, torn into pieces.

KITCHARI

SERVES 2
PREPARATION TIME 10 minutes
COOKING TIME 1 hour–1 hour and 10 minutes
+ resting

100 g (3½ oz) green mung
   beans, rinsed and soaked
   overnight
1 litre (1¾ pints) water
1 teaspoon ground turmeric
¼ teaspoon ground black
   pepper
1 sheet of kombu seaweed
   or ¼ teaspoon asafoetida
20 g (¾ oz) butter
¼ teaspoon mustard seeds
¼ teaspoon cumin seeds
¼ teaspoon fennel seeds
¼ teaspoon nigella seeds
6 dried curry leaves
zest and juice of 1 lemon
sea salt flakes

**FOR THE CRISPY ONIONS
(OPTIONAL)**
vegetable oil, for frying
1 onion, sliced into rings
plain flour, for dusting

TO SERVE
natural yogurt
chopped nuts
spiced & roasted seeds
   (see page 141)
pea shoots

Rinse the soaked mung beans a couple of times, then drain and put into a saucepan with the measured water.

Add the turmeric, black pepper and seaweed or asafoetida and bring to the boil. Reduce to a low simmer and cook for about 1 hour, or until the beans are soft.

Melt the butter in a frying pan over a medium heat and, when bubbling, add the seeds, curry leaves and lemon zest. When the seeds begin to pop, remove from the heat and carefully add to the kitchari. Add the lemon juice and sea salt to taste.

Take the kitchari off the heat, then cover and rest for 5–10 minutes while you prepare the crispy onions, if using.

Heat the oil in a wok over a high heat. Dip the onion rings in flour and carefully lower a few at a time into the hot oil using tongs. When they are golden and crispy remove from the pan and drain on kitchen paper.

Serve the kitchari in bowls, topped with any or all of the serving suggestions listed

COCONUT CHICKEN SOUP WITH TURMERIC & KALE

SERVES 2
PREPARATION TIME 10 minutes
COOKING TIME about 15–20 minutes

1 tablespoon coconut oil
1 small onion, chopped
200 ml (7 fl oz) coconut water
200 ml (7 fl oz) chicken stock (see pages 7–9)
1 teaspoon grated fresh turmeric or ground turmeric
¼ teaspoon ground black pepper

100 g (3½ oz) kale, stalks removed and leaves shredded
1 baby gem lettuce, halved
1 tablespoon olive oil
100 g (3½ oz) leftover roast chicken
squeeze of lemon juice, to taste (optional)
sea salt flakes

Melt half the coconut oil in a heavy-based saucepan and sauté the onion over a medium heat for 8–10 minutes until soft. Add the coconut water, stock, turmeric and black pepper. Keep at a low simmer.

Heat the remaining coconut oil in a frying pan or wok and sauté the kale with a good pinch of sea salt for a few minutes until softened.

Place a griddle pan over a high heat, brush the lettuce halves with the olive oil and griddle on both sides for 2–3 minutes.

Divide the kale, lettuce and chicken between bowls and pour over the hot coconut chicken stock. Taste and add lemon juice, if using. Serve immediately.

VEG-FORWARD

CELERIAC & APPLE SOUP

SERVES 6
PREPARATION TIME 10–15 minutes
COOKING TIME 20–25 minutes

25 g (1 oz) butter or margarine
1 celeriac (about 500 g / 1 lb),
  peeled and coarsely grated
3 dessert apples, peeled, cored
  and chopped
1.2 litres (2 pints) vegetable
  stock (see pages 7–9)

pinch of cayenne pepper,
  or more to taste
salt

TO GARNISH
2–3 tablespoons finely diced
  dessert apple
paprika

Melt the butter or margarine in a large saucepan and cook
the celeriac and apples over a moderate heat for 5 minutes,
or until they have begun to soften.

Add the stock and cayenne pepper and bring to the
boil. Reduce the heat, cover the pan and simmer for
15–20 minutes, or until the celeriac and apples are soft.

Purée the mixture in a blender or food processor until it
is very smooth, transferring each batch to a clean saucepan.
Alternatively, rub through a fine sieve.

Reheat gently. Season to taste and serve in bowls,
garnished with the apple and a dusting of paprika.

CORIANDER & LENTIL SOUP

SERVES 8
PREPARATION TIME 10–15 minutes
COOKING TIME 40–50 minutes

500 g (1 lb) dried red lentils, rinsed
2 tablespoons vegetable oil
2 onions, chopped
2 garlic cloves, chopped
2 celery sticks, chopped
400 g (13 oz) can chopped tomatoes, drained
1 teaspoon paprika
1 teaspoon harissa paste
1 teaspoon ground cumin
1.2 litres (2 pints) vegetable stock (see pages 7–9)
salt and pepper
2 tablespoons chopped coriander, to garnish

Heat the oil in a large saucepan and gently fry the onions, garlic and celery over a low heat until softened.

Add the lentils to the vegetable pan along with the tomatoes. Mix well. Add the paprika, harissa paste, cumin and vegetable stock and season with salt and pepper. Cover the pan and simmer gently for 40–50 minutes until the lentils are tender, adding a little hot water if the soup gets too thick.

Serve the soup immediately in warmed bowls topped with a little chopped coriander.

SPICY CORIANDER & WHITE BEAN SOUP

SERVES 8
PREPARATION TIME 10–15 minutes
COOKING TIME 40–50 minutes

2 tablespoons vegetable oil
2 onions, chopped
2 garlic cloves, chopped
2 celery sticks, chopped
2 x 425 g (14 oz) cans of
 haricot or cannellini beans,
 drained and rinsed
1 chilli, chopped
1 teaspoon paprika
1 teaspoon harissa paste

1 teaspoon ground cumin
1.2 litres (2 pints) vegetable
 stock (see pages 7–9)
salt and pepper

TO GARNISH
2 tablespoons chopped
 coriander
4 tablespoons chopped
 parsley

Heat the oil in a large saucepan and gently fry the onions,
garlic and celery over a low heat until softened.

Add the beans to the pan with the chilli, paprika, harissa
paste, cumin and vegetable stock, and season with salt and
pepper. Cover the pan and simmer gently for 40–50 minutes,
then roughly mash some of the beans to thicken the soup.
Finish with the chopped herbs and serve immediately in
warmed bowls.

CELERIAC & ROASTED GARLIC SOUP

SERVES 6
PREPARATION TIME 10–15 minutes
COOKING TIME 20–25 minutes

25 g (1 oz) butter or margarine
1 celeriac (about 500 g / 1 lb), peeled and grated
1 onion, chopped
2 garlic bulbs
1 litre (1¾ pints) of vegetable stock (see pages 7–9)

pinch of cayenne pepper
salt
150 ml (¼ pint) milk

TO SERVE
double cream
paprika

Melt the butter or margarine in a large saucepan and cook the celeriac and onion over a moderate heat for 5 minutes, or until they have begun to soften.

Take the garlic out of their papery skins, add to the celeriac along with the stock, cayenne pepper and salt and bring to the boil. Reduce the heat, cover the pan and simmer for 15–20 minutes, or until the celeriac is soft.

Purée the mixture in a blender or food processor until it is very smooth, transferring each batch to a clean saucepan. Alternatively, rub through a fine sieve.

Reheat gently with the milk, then serve with a little double cream in each bowl and a dusting of paprika.

GARDEN HERB SOUP

SERVES 4
PREPARATION TIME 15 minutes
COOKING TIME 30 minutes

50 g (2 oz) butter
1 onion, roughly chopped
1 baking potato
   (about 250 g / 8 oz), diced
1 litre (1¾ pints) vegetable
   stock (see pages 7–9)

75 g (3 oz) mixed parsley and
   chives, roughly torn into
   pieces
salt and pepper

Heat the butter in a saucepan, add the onion and fry gently for 5 minutes until softened but not browned. Add the potato, tossing it into the butter then cover and fry gently for 10 minutes, stirring occasionally until just turning golden around the edges.

Add the stock, season with salt and pepper and bring to the boil. Cover and simmer for 10 minutes, or until the potato is tender. Cool slightly, then purée in batches in a blender or food processor with the herbs.

Pour back into the saucepan, reheat, then taste and adjust the seasoning if needed. Serve in mugs with a side of toasted bacon sandwiches.

CREAMY CAULIFLOWER & CASHEW SOUP

SERVES 6
PREPARATION TIME 25 minutes
COOKING TIME 25 minutes

1 tablespoon sunflower oil
25 g (1 oz) butter
1 onion, roughly chopped
50 g (2 oz) cashew nuts
1 cauliflower, cut into florets,
   woody core discarded
   (about 500 g / 1 lb when
   prepared)
900 ml (1½ pints) vegetable
   stock (see pages 7–9)

nutmeg, grated
300 ml (½ pint) milk
150 ml (¼ pint) double cream
salt and pepper

FOR THE HONEY-
GLAZED CASHEWS
5 g (½ oz) butter
50 g (2 oz) cashew nuts
1 tablespoon honey

Heat the oil and butter in a saucepan, add the onion and cashew nuts and fry for 5 minutes until the onion is softened and the nuts very lightly coloured. Stir in the cauliflower florets, then the stock. Season with salt, pepper and a little grated nutmeg and bring to the boil.

Cover and simmer for 15 minutes until the cauliflower is just tender.

Meanwhile, make the glazed nuts. Heat the butter in a frying pan, add the nuts and cook until pale golden, stirring until lightly browned. Add the honey and cook for a further 1–2 minutes until golden and caramelized. Set aside until ready to serve.

Purée the cooked soup in batches in a blender or food processor, then pour back into the saucepan and stir in the milk and half the cream. Bring just to the boil, then taste and adjust the seasoning if needed.

Ladle the soup into shallow bowls, drizzle over the remaining cream and sprinkle with the glazed nuts.

GINGERED CAULIFLOWER SOUP

SERVES 6
PREPARATION TIME 25 minutes
COOKING TIME 25 minutes

1 tablespoon sunflower oil
25 g (1 oz) butter
1 onion, roughly chopped
1 cauliflower, cut into florets,
    woody core discarded
    (about 500 g / 1 lb when
    prepared)
3.5 cm (1½ inch) piece root
    ginger, peeled and finely
    chopped
900 ml (1½ pints) vegetable
    stock (see pages 7–9)

300 ml (½ pint) milk
150 ml (¼ pint) double cream
salt and pepper

SOY-GLAZED SEEDS
1 tablespoon sunflower oil
2 tablespoons sesame seeds
2 tablespoons sunflower
    seeds
2 tablespoons pumpkin seeds
1 tablespoon soy sauce

Heat the oil and butter in a saucepan, add the onion and fry for 5 minutes until softened but not coloured. Stir in the cauliflower florets and ginger, then the stock. Season with salt and pepper and bring to the boil.

Cover and simmer for 15 minutes until the cauliflower is just tender.

Meanwhile, make the glazed seeds. Heat the oil in a frying pan, add the seeds and cook for 2–3 minutes, stirring until lightly browned. Add the soy sauce, then quickly cover the pan with a lid until the seeds have stopped popping. Set aside until ready to serve.

Purée the cooked soup in batches in a blender or food processor, then pour back into the saucepan and stir in the milk and half the cream. Bring just to the boil, then taste and adjust the seasoning if needed.

Ladle the soup into shallow bowls, drizzle over the remaining cream and sprinkle with some of the glazed seeds, serving the remaining seeds in a small bowl for further sprinkling.

CAULIFLOWER SOUP WITH MATCHA MIMOSA

SERVES 4
PREPARATION TIME 10 minutes
COOKING TIME about 25 minutes

1 tablespoon unsalted
butter
1 large cauliflower, cut
into florets
¾ teaspoon matcha powder
500 ml (18 fl oz) unsweetened
almond milk

250 ml (9 fl oz) vegetable
stock (see pages 7–9)
2 eggs
½ celery stick, finely chopped
1 teaspoon dried oregano
sea salt
sesame oil, for drizzling

Heat the butter in a large saucepan, add the cauliflower and a good pinch of salt and sauté over a medium–high heat for a few minutes.

Add ½ teaspoon of the matcha powder, then the milk and stock. Bring to the boil and simmer for 10–15 minutes, or until the cauliflower is cooked. Transfer to a blender and whizz until smooth (or use a hand-held blender). Taste for and adjust the seasoning if needed.

Meanwhile, add the eggs to a pan of boiling water and boil for 8 minutes. Cool them under running water, then peel and chop. Mix together with the celery, the remaining matcha powder, oregano and a little salt.

Ladle the soup into bowls, drizzle with sesame oil and top with the matcha mimosa.

MATCHA MUSHROOM NOODLE SOUP

SERVES 2
PREPARATION TIME 5 minutes + overnight soaking
COOKING TIME about 10 minutes

10 g (½oz) dried shiitake
   mushrooms
400 ml (14 fl oz) water
200 g (7 oz) udon noodles
2 tablespoons soy sauce
1 tablespoon mirin

1 tablespoon sesame oil
100 g (3½ oz) fresh enoki or
   shiitake mushrooms
1 teaspoon matcha powder
100 g (3½ oz) baby spinach
   leaves, shredded

To make the mushroom dashi (stock) for the soup, soak the dried mushrooms in the measured water overnight.

When you are ready to make the soup, bring the mushroom dashi to the boil in a saucepan, along with the soaked mushrooms. Add the noodles, soy sauce and mirin and cook for 4–5 minutes.

At the same time, heat the sesame oil in a frying pan and add the fresh mushrooms. Sprinkle with the matcha powder and cook over a medium–high heat for 2 minutes. Add the spinach, stir through to wilt slightly, then remove from the heat.

Divide the mushrooms and spinach between the bowls and ladle over the noodle broth.

ROASTED PUMPKIN, TOMATO & SAGE SOUP

SERVES 4
PREPARATION TIME 10 minutes
COOKING TIME 15–20 minutes

875 g (1¾ lb) pumpkin or butternut squash, peeled, halved, deseeded and cut into 1.5 cm (¾ inch) cubes
50 ml (2 fl oz) olive oil
600 ml (1 pint) vegetable stock (see pages 7–9)
200 ml (7 fl oz) passata
1 tablespoon finely chopped sage leaves
100 ml (3½ fl oz) double cream
salt and pepper

Place the pumpkin into a small roasting tin, drizzle over 2 tablespoons of the oil, season with salt and pepper, and toss to mix well. Roast in a preheated oven, 220°C (425°F), Gas Mark 7, for 15–20 minutes, or until just tender.

Add the roasted pumpkin into a saucepan with the stock, passata and sage. Bring to the boil, then reduce the heat and simmer for 12–15 minutes. Using a hand-held blender, whizz the mixture until smooth. Stir in the double cream and serve with warmed crusty bread.

PESTO & LEMON SOUP

SERVES 6
PREPARATION TIME 10 minutes
COOKING TIME 25 minutes

1 tablespoon olive oil
1 onion, finely chopped
2 garlic cloves, finely chopped
2 tomatoes, skinned and
    chopped
1.2 litres (2 pints) vegetable
    stock (see pages 7–9)
3 teaspoons green pesto, plus
    extra to serve
rind and juice of 1 lemon

100 g (3½ oz) broccoli, cut into
    small florets
150 g (5 oz) courgette, diced
100 g (3½ oz) frozen green
    soya beans
65 g (2½ oz) small pasta shapes
50 g (2 oz) spinach, shredded
salt and pepper
basil leaves, to garnish

Heat the oil in a saucepan, add the onion and fry gently for
5 minutes, stirring occasionally, until softened. Add the
garlic, tomatoes, stock, pesto, lemon rind and salt and
pepper, to taste, and simmer for 10 minutes.

Add the broccoli, courgette, soya beans and pasta shapes,
then simmer for 6 minutes. Add the spinach and lemon juice
and cook for 2 minutes until the spinach has just wilted and
the pasta is cooked.

Ladle into bowls, top with extra spoonfuls of pesto and
garnish with a sprinkling of basil leaves.

SPRING VEGETABLE BROTH

SERVES 4
PREPARATION TIME 15 minutes
COOKING TIME 30–35 minutes

2 teaspoons olive oil
2 celery sticks with their
    leaves, chopped
2 leeks, chopped
1 carrot, finely diced
50 g (2 oz) pearl barley

1.2 litres (2 pints) vegetable
    stock (see pages 7–9)
1 teaspoon English mustard
125 g (4 oz) mangetout, sliced
    diagonally (optional)
salt and pepper

Heat the oil in a saucepan and add the celery, leeks and carrot. Cook over a medium heat for 5 minutes.

Stir in the pearl barley, stock and mustard, season to taste and simmer for 20–25 minutes. Add the mangetout, if liked, and simmer for 5 minutes.

Ladle into warmed bowls and serve piping hot.

SWEETCORN & CELERY SOUP WITH CHILLI & TOMATO CHUTNEY

SERVES 6
PREPARATION TIME 25 minutes
COOKING TIME 30 minutes

50 g (2 oz) butter
1 onion, chopped
4 corn on the cob, green leaves removed, kernels cut from cobs
3 celery sticks, sliced
2 garlic cloves, finely chopped
1 litre (1¾ pints) vegetable stock (see pages 7–9)
2 bay leaves
salt and cayenne pepper

FOR THE CHILLI & TOMATO CHUTNEY
1 tablespoon sunflower oil
½ red onion, finely chopped
1 red pepper, cored, deseeded and diced
1–2 large mild red chillies, cored, deseeded and finely chopped
4 tomatoes, chopped (skinned, if preferred)
4 tablespoons caster sugar
2 tablespoons red wine vinegar
salt and pepper

Heat the butter in a saucepan, add the onion and fry gently for 5 minutes until just beginning to turn golden around the edges. Add the corn, celery and garlic and fry for 5 minutes.

Pour in the stock, add the bay leaves, and season with salt and cayenne pepper, then bring to the boil. Cover and simmer for 20 minutes.

Discard the bay leaves, then allow the soup to cool slightly. Purée the soup in batches in a blender or food processor until smooth. Return to the saucepan and reheat. Taste and adjust the seasoning if needed.

Make the chilli and tomato chutney. Heat the sunflower oil in a small saucepan, add the onion, pepper and chillies and fry gently for 5 minutes until softened, then mix in the tomatoes, sugar, vinegar and salt and pepper to taste. Simmer for 15 minutes, stirring occasionally, until thick.

Ladle the soup into bowls and top with spoonfuls of the chilli and tomato chutney.

GARLICKY BROTHY CHICKPEAS WITH TOMATO & CHILLI

SERVES 2
PREPARATION TIME 10 minutes
COOKING TIME about 15 minutes

2 tablespoons olive oil,
plus extra for drizzling
1 onion, finely chopped
250 g (8 oz) cherry
tomatoes, halved
1 red chilli, deseeded and
finely chopped

3 garlic cloves, crushed
400 g (13 oz) can chickpeas
500 ml (17 fl oz) vegetable
stock (see pages 7–9)
salt and pepper

Heat the oil in a medium saucepan, add the onion, tomatoes, chilli and garlic and cook over a medium heat for at least 8 minutes until the tomatoes have cooked down.

Add the chickpeas and their liquid from the can, and the stock. Season with salt and pepper to taste. Bring to a simmer and cook for 2 minutes.

Serve in bowls, drizzled with olive oil and topped with a grinding of pepper.

GARLICKY BROTHY BEANS WITH RAINBOW CHARD

SERVES 2
PREPARATION TIME 10 minutes
COOKING TIME about 15 minutes

2 tablespoons olive oil,
plus extra for drizzling
1 onion, finely chopped
3 garlic cloves, crushed
150 g (5 oz) rainbow chard,
stalks cut into 1 cm (½ inch)
thick slices and leaves
roughly chopped

400 g (13 oz) can cannellini
or other beans
finely grated zest and juice of
1 lemon
500 ml (17 fl oz) vegetable
stock (see pages 7–9)
salt and pepper

Heat the oil in a saucepan, add the onion and cook over a medium heat for 8 minutes until softened.

Stir in the garlic and rainbow chard stalks and cook for another 2 minutes. Add the beans and their liquid from the can, the lemon zest and juice and stock. Season with salt and pepper to taste. Bring to a simmer, then add the rainbow chard leaves and cook for 2 minutes.

Serve in bowls, drizzled with olive oil and topped with a grinding of pepper.

MISO VEGETABLE & PASTA SOUP

SERVES 4–6
PREPARATION TIME 15 minutes
COOKING TIME about 20 minutes

3 tablespoons olive oil, plus extra for drizzling
1 large onion, finely chopped
2 carrots, peeled and finely chopped
2 celery sticks, finely chopped
2 garlic cloves, crushed
2 litres (3½ pints) water
2 tablespoons white miso paste
100 g (3½ oz) spaghetti, broken into small pieces
2 courgettes, cut into small pieces
½ hispi (sweetheart) cabbage, finely shredded
4 tomatoes, cut into small pieces
200 g (7 oz) asparagus spears, cut into 1 cm (½ inch) slices on the diagonal
400 g (13 oz) can borlotti or haricot beans, drained and rinsed
finely grated zest and juice of 1 lemon
salt and pepper

Heat the oil in a large saucepan, add the onion, carrots, celery and garlic and cook over a medium heat for about 8 minutes until the onion is soft and translucent.

Pour over the measured water, add the miso paste and stir to dissolve. Bring to a simmer, add the spaghetti and cook for 5 minutes. Stir in the courgettes and cabbage and cook for another 5 minutes.

Add the tomatoes, asparagus, beans, lemon zest and juice, and salt and pepper to taste and cook for another 2 minutes. Add more water if you prefer it more brothy.

Serve in bowls, drizzled with olive oil and seasoned with extra salt and pepper, if needed.

MATCHA BUCKWHEAT BROTH

SERVES 2
PREPARATION TIME 10 minutes
COOKING TIME about 20 minutes

600 ml (1 pint) vegetable
stock (see pages 7–9)
1 lemongrass stalk, bashed
100 g (3½ oz) buckwheat
1 tablespoon coconut oil
100 g (3½ oz) cavolo nero or
kale, stalks removed and
leaves shredded

1 teaspoon grated root ginger
½ teaspoon matcha powder
2 tablespoons wheat-free
tamari soy sauce

Bring the stock to the boil in a saucepan. Add the
lemongrass and buckwheat, reduce to a simmer and cook
for about 10 minutes, or until the buckwheat is tender.

Meanwhile, heat the coconut oil in a frying pan or wok,
add the greens, ginger and matcha powder and sauté for
about 5 minutes, adding the soy sauce just as the greens
become tender.

Discard the lemongrass and divide the broth between
bowls, topping with the ginger matcha greens.

SPICED WATERCRESS & MATCHA SOUP

SERVES 4
PREPARATION TIME 10 minutes
COOKING TIME about 20 minutes

1 tablespoon olive oil
1 leek, sliced
2 teaspoons matcha powder
pinch of cayenne pepper
pinch of ground cloves
¼ teaspoon ground ginger
¼ teaspoon ground coriander
¼ teaspoon ground cardamom

½ teaspoon grated nutmeg
350 g (12 oz) spinach
150 g (5½ oz) watercress, plus extra to garnish
½ teaspoon sea salt
good pinch of black pepper
600 ml (1 pint) hot vegetable stock (see pages 7–9)

Heat the oil in a saucepan and add the leek. Sauté over a medium heat for 10 minutes until soft. Add the matcha powder and all the ground spices, stirring and cooking for another 5 minutes.

Add the spinach, watercress, salt and pepper and stir through, then add the stock and stir just until the leaves have wilted. Use a hand-held blender to blitz as soon as possible in order to retain the bright green colour. Garnish with extra watercress.

SCATTER, DUNK & DIP

FENNEL FLATBREADS

MAKES 6
PREPARATION TIME 30 minutes
COOKING TIME 2½ hours

200 g (7 oz) self-raising flour,
   plus extra for dusting
½ teaspoon baking powder
1 teaspoon fennel seeds,
   roughly crushed

2 tablespoons olive oil
6–7 tablespoons water
salt and pepper

Place flour and baking powder into a bowl, add the fennel seeds, oil and a little salt and pepper, then gradually mix in the measured water to make a soft dough.

Cut the dough into 6 pieces, then roll each piece out on a lightly floured surface into a rough oval shape about the size of a hand. Cook on a preheated ridged frying pan for 3–4 minutes each side until singed and puffy. Serve warm or cold with soup.

GARLIC CROÛTONS

SERVES 4–6
PREPARATION TIME 5 minutes
COOKING TIME about 5 minutes

6–8 slices of white or brown
bread, crusts removed

6–8 tablespoons olive oil
3 garlic cloves, sliced

Cut the bread into 1 cm (½ inch) cubes. Heat the oil in a large frying pan, add the garlic and cook over a moderate heat for 1 minute. Add the bread and fry, turning frequently, until evenly golden brown.

Drain the croûtons on a plate lined with kitchen paper. Serve as a crunchy, delicious soup topping.

SALT & PEPPER GRISSINI

MAKES 18
PREPARATION TIME 15 minutes + proving
COOKING TIME 6–8 minutes

250 g (8 oz) strong white flour, plus extra for dusting

¼ teaspoon salt

1 teaspoon caster sugar

1 teaspoon fast-action dried yeast

4 teaspoons olive oil, plus extra for oiling

150 ml (¼ pint) warm water

1 egg, beaten

coarse sea salt

black peppercorns, roughly crushed

Place the flour into a bowl and mix with the salt, sugar and yeast. Add the oil and gradually mix in the measured water until you've made a smooth dough.

Knead for 5 minutes on a lightly floured surface, then cut the dough into 18 pieces and roll each into a thin rope. Put on a greased baking sheet, cover with oiled clingfilm and leave in a warm place to rise for 30 minutes.

Remove the clingfilm, brush the bread with beaten egg, then sprinkle with a little coarse sea salt and a generous scattering of black peppercorns.

Bake in a preheated oven, 200°C (400°F), Gas Mark 6, for 6–8 minutes until golden. Serve warm or cold with soup.

BABY WALNUT SCONES

MAKES about 10
PREPARATION TIME 10 minutes
COOKING TIME 10–12 minutes

50 g (2 oz) butter, plus extra
   for greasing
250 g (8 oz) self-raising flour
50 g (2 oz) walnuts, roughly
   chopped
2 teaspoons thyme leaves

75 g (3 oz) mature Cheddar,
   grated
1 egg, beaten
8–10 tablespoons milk
salt and pepper

Rub the butter into the flour. Season and mix in the walnuts, thyme leaves and cheese. Mix in half the beaten egg and all the milk to make a soft dough.

Knead lightly, then roll out to 2.5 cm (1 inch) thickness. Stamp out about ten 5 cm (2 inch) circles.

Put on a greased baking sheet and brush with the remaining egg. Bake in a preheated oven, 200°C (400°F), Gas Mark 6, for 10–12 minutes. Serve warm with soup.

COURGETTE MUFFINS

MAKES 12
PREPARATION TIME 10 minutes
COOKING TIME 18–20 minutes

300 g (10 oz) self-raising flour
3 teaspoons baking powder
75 g (3 oz) vegetarian
    Parmesan, grated
200 g (7 oz) courgette,
    coarsely grated

150 ml (5 oz) natural yogurt
3 tablespoons olive oil
3 eggs
3 tablespoons milk

Place the flour into a bowl, and add baking powder, Parmesan, courgette, yogurt, oil, eggs and milk.

Fork together until just mixed, and divide into a 12-hole muffin tin lined with paper cases.

Bake in a preheated oven, 200°C (400°F), Gas Mark 6, for 18–20 minutes until well risen and golden brown. Serve warm with soup.

PARMESAN THINS

MAKES 18
PREPARATION TIME 5 minutes
COOKING TIME 5 minutes

100 g (3½ oz) Parmesan, grated

Line a baking sheet with non-stick baking paper, then sprinkle the Parmesan into 18 well-spaced mounds.

Cook in a preheated oven, 190°C (375°F), Gas Mark 5, for about 5 minutes, or until the cheese has melted and is just beginning to brown.

Leave to cool and harden, then peel off the paper and serve on the side with soup.

PARMESAN
TWISTS

MAKES about 25
PREPARATION TIME 5 minutes
COOKING TIME 10 minutes

425 g (14 oz) ready-rolled
   puff pastry, defrosted if
   frozen
1 egg yolk, beaten
3 teaspoons green or red
   pesto

pinch of black pepper
4 tablespoons Parmesan,
   grated
olive oil, for oiling

Unroll one sheet of pastry from a pack of 2 sheets.

Brush with a little beaten egg yolk, then spread with the pesto, season with pepper and sprinkle over the Parmesan. Cover with the second unrolled pastry sheet.

Brush the top with a little more egg yolk, then cut into strips about 1 cm (½ inch) wide. Twist each strip like a corkscrew, transfer to an oiled baking sheet and press the ends firmly on to the baking sheet to prevent them unravelling.

Cook in a preheated oven, 200°C (400°F), Gas Mark 6, for about 10 minutes until golden brown. Serve warm with soup.

MELBA TOAST

MAKES 8
PREPARATION TIME 5 minutes
COOKING TIME about 5 minutes

4 slices of bread

Lightly toast the bread on both sides. Trim off the crusts and discard, then splice each slice with a sharp knife to make 8 very thin slices.

Cut the slices into triangles, then put on a baking sheet, untoasted side upwards and grill until the corners of the bread begin to curl. Serve on the side with soup.

SPICED &
ROASTED SEEDS

MAKES 200 G (7 oz)
PREPARATION TIME 5 minutes
COOKING TIME 30–40 minutes

100 g (3½ oz) pumpkin seeds
100 g (3½ oz) sunflower seeds
1 tablespoon olive oil
juice of 1 lime

juice of 1 orange
½ teaspoon ground turmeric
½ teaspoon mild chilli powder
½ teaspoon sea salt flakes

Mix all the ingredients together in a bowl, then spread out a baking tray lined with baking paper. Roast in a preheated the oven, 180°C (350°F), Gas Mark 4, for 30–40 minutes, shaking the seeds halfway through cooking, until golden and crunchy.

Allow to cool, then transfer to an airtight jar.

Serve as a crunchy, delicious soup topping.

RECIPES INDEX

**Recipes are marked as
being suitable for vegans
(vg) or vegetarians (v)**

UK/US GLOSSARY

UK	US
baking tray	baking sheet
chickpea	garbanzo
chilli	chili
chilli flakes	red pepper flakes
clingfilm	plastic wrap
coriander	cilantro
cornflour	cornstarch
courgette	zucchini
cream (double)	heavy cream
flour (plain)	all-purpose
flour (self-raising)	self-rising
frying pan	skillet
gram flour	chickpea flour
grill	broil
hob	stove
jug	pitcher
kitchen paper	paper towels
natural yogurt	plain yogurt
prawn	shrimp
ridicchio	chicory
sieve	strainer
spring onion	scallion
stoned	pitted
sugar (caster)	superfine
sweetcorn	corn
tomato purée	tomato paste

PUBLISHER'S NOTE:

Standard level spoon measurements are used in all recipes.

1 tablespoon = one 15 ml spoon
1 teaspoon = one 5 ml spoon

Both imperial and metric measurements have been given in all recipes. Use one set of measurements only and not a mixture of both.

Eggs should be medium unless otherwise stated. The Department of Health advises that eggs should not be consumed raw. This book contains dishes made with raw or lightly cooked eggs. It is prudent for more vulnerable people such as pregnant and nursing mothers, the elderly, babies and young children to avoid uncooked or lightly cooked dishes made with eggs. Once prepared these dishes should be kept refrigerated and used promptly.

Milk should be full fat unless otherwise stated.

Fresh herbs should be used unless otherwise stated. If unavailable use dried herbs as an alternative but halve the quantities stated.

Ovens should be preheated to the specific temperature – if using a fan-assisted oven, follow manufacturer's instructions for adjusting the time and the temperature.

Pepper should be freshly ground black pepper unless otherwise stated.

This book includes dishes made with nuts and nut derivatives. It is advisable for customers with known allergic reactions to nuts and nut derivatives and those who may be potentially vulnerable to these allergies, such as babies and children with a family history of allergies, to avoid dishes made with nuts and nut oils. It is also prudent to check the labels of pre-prepared ingredients for the possible inclusion of nut derivatives.

Vegetarians should look for the 'V' symbol on a cheese to ensure it is made with vegetarian rennet.

ALSO AVAILABLE

Recipes for Pickling & Preserving

Recipes for Savoury Bakes

Recipes for Summer